GIVE YOUR BEST

HOW WILLEM CHARLES TRANSFORMED HIS HAITIAN VILLAGE FROM POVERTY IN VOODOO TO PROSPERITY IN CHRISTIANITY

ANDREW DEWITT

TABLE OF CONTENTS

ACKNOWLEDGEMENTS

When I first met Willem in the summer of 2002, I heard him speak, and after listening for a period of time, I thought, "How come nobody has written a book about this man's life?" A few years have passed, and I have been able to spend countless hours with Willem and his lovely wife, Beth. The process of creating this book was a project that took the cooperation of numerous individuals from various regions of the United States, Canada, and Haiti. At the risk of leaving out important names, I will do my best to mention many of those who donated their time and energy to this effort.

First, I would like to thank my incredible wife who put up with my endless hours at the computer. In addition to all the normal work she does on a routine basis, she took up duties that are normally mine like shoveling snow and mowing grass so that I could complete this book. Not only that, but she also worked as my initial copyeditor and chief cheerleader.

Next, I need to thank my parents who have been my inspiration for everything having to do with mission work since I was a child. They exemplify a servant's heart as they tirelessly volunteer their time, talents, and treasure working to advance the kingdom of God. Their heart for mission work has taken them to six continents, and their writing and editing talent has inspired me to record my thoughts since I was young. My mother's editorial services have not only been crucial for improvement of this text but have encouraged to me to continue to bring this story to life.

Those involved in Willem's life as a young man provided copious information about his personality and experiences as a youth. The stories ranged in their feeling from tragic to hilarious, including everything in between. They were shared between episodes of tears and guffaws as memories were exhumed. Many of the early supporters of Mountain Top Ministries (MTM) took risks with a young organization and made the dream a reality. I would like to acknowledge Dave Smittson, John Townsend, Jerry Poppe, Judy Tharpe, Michelle Wilmot, Roger Gingerich, Nancy Gangwer, Nancy Lopshire, Josh Person, Leroy Steury, Tammy Steury, Larry Neese Jr., Larry Neese Sr., Jeff Lammey, Bill Rolfson, David Jones, John Chorpenning, Ron Ediger, Mike Shatto, Barry Cowen, Bob Johnson, Sharon Johnson, Brad Johnson, Deb Williams, and Angie Francis.

The mission teams who have served at MTM have always been near and dear to my heart. I've truly enjoyed working side by side with every member of each team of which I've been a part. A number of people have contributed to this book in ways that they might not even be aware of, and I would like to thank Marcia Favali, Shanu Kothari, Tami Gudenkauf, Deb Ihde, Lori Webb, Joe Fuller, Sue Walsh, Peg Kothari, Kris Tiernan, Jane Gandy, Michael Bruce Lyle, James Matheos, Brian Pendleton, Darrell Cloud, and Fran Baker.

A number of pastors and friends have brought me guidance and education in my personal development and understanding about mission work. With their solid biblical foundation, I have been able to formulate a Christ-centered philosophy of ministry partnerships and mission work. I thank Boyd Baker, Marv Feigenspan, Gene Reynolds, Lee Armstrong, Terry Bemis, Matt Collins, and Roger Stroup.

A number of Haitians were very helpful in the process of gathering information about Willem's life as well as Haitian schools, churches, and culture. I appreciate the time spent with Rachael Denache McIntosh, Bernard Angus, Mme. Stephen, and Johanne Fethier.

In the process of interviewing and writing, I have done my best to tell stories accurately and in a way that conveys a message. On occasion, I've condensed or combined events for simplicity, but the core message remains unchanged.

Most of all, I want to honor the Lord Jesus Christ as I recall the stories in this book. My goal is that everything herein points to Christ.

PREFACE

Give Your Best introduces Mountain Top Ministries (MTM) through the voice of the ministry's founder and leader, Willem Charles as he tells the story while driving across Haitian roads up to the village of Gramothe. After getting an understanding of the setting, we learn about Willem's early life. His childhood, early successes and failures in business, his work as a translator for CNN, and participation on Haiti's National Soccer Team provide him with an unusual breadth of experience. In order to understand Willem's homeland better, we walk through a brief history of Haiti that sheds light on some of the overall problems the country faces.

Willem's conversion to Christianity leads him to a missionary base where his skills are recognized, and he quickly becomes the right hand man for the American missionary in charge. After many years of experience and many lessons learned there, he is called to start MTM in the village of Gramothe, Haiti. His theme in everything he does is to Give Your Best. This call for excellence reverberates in different forms through various stories of MTM's origins. The stories of the water project, the trailer, the church, the schools, and the medical clinic demonstrate his relentless pursuit of excellence as he lives out his calling by delivering the message Jesus Christ and sounding the call for supporters to honor God's children by always giving their best.

On January 12, 2010, a devastating earthquake rocked Haiti. The epilogue discusses the initial destruction to the country, the international response, and how the disaster affected MTM.

All proceeds from the sale of this book will go to support the work of MTM in Haiti.

CHAPTER 1
INTRODUCTION

I lift up my eyes to the hills—where does my help come from?
My help comes from the LORD, the maker of heaven and earth.

Psalm 121:1-2

Willem Charles drove the fifteen-year-old red Chevy pickup through the gate outside his home. It took about ten minutes to slowly lumber down the half mile of semipaved road to arrive at the river at the bottom of the mountain. This Haitian road had been paved once, many years ago. The scattered remnants of concrete now served more as hindrances to movement rather than functional pavement. They would test the ability of any two-wheel-drive car but were no match for this four-wheel-drive Chevy. Looking out the window, we saw people everywhere. Men and women huddled in doorways, seated along the road, and just standing in groups without any direction or place to go. Barefoot children gathered together on porches and played with sticks along the side of the road. Their faces were void of any expression, and they simply stared at the foreigners passing by in the truck. Willem explained that the schools were only for those who could afford it, and jobs are so scarce. Most of these people never were able to attend school and most didn't have jobs. Poverty was their way of life.

The serpentine road leveled off just before reaching the Petit Riveire de Nippes at the bottom of the hillside. We looked across the riverbed and saw the steep but fertile ground sloping up on the opposite side. Slowly, Willem pointed the Chevy into the riverbed and surprisingly, there was very little water. While the riverbed was over 200 feet wide, water only coursed through a few areas, which meant that only about ten feet of the river required actual water crossing. The truck followed a path that had been carved into the smooth, white river rocks by numerous similar crossings. As he drove into the water, Willem began the story of how he started Mountain Top Ministries.

"I was born just right over there," he said, pointing behind and to the right of our current location in Thomassin forty-eight, Haiti. "I grew up here and know this place like the back of my hand. Back about ten years ago, voodoo temples were everywhere; most people didn't have a hope of ever getting a career. Most people would go through their day with the single worry about where to get their next meal. This was their main focus every single day. Ninety percent of the people in this village were unemployed. There was nothing here except for the five voodoo temples. But my thing is God called me to this place, and he told me to start a ministry in this village."

The village of Gramothe occupied the hillside just opposite Willem's home. With no running water, no electricity, no school, and no buildings or even any businesses of significance, Gramothe was primitive. Yet, 2,500 people called the village home and struggled to subsist day to day.

"I went over to the village and looked around," Willem said in his thick Haitian accent as he pulled the truck out of the river and onto the road on the other side. "There was a small group of kids gathered around a lady who was teaching them," he said. Willem shook his head and continued. "I knew her, and she only had a third-grade education. She was not qualified to be a teacher in any way. But this was their school for the village, taught by a lady who needed school herself. I spent some time over there and talked to the elders of the village. After a while I told them, 'I'm going to start a church and a school here.' The men in the village just laughed at me. Time and time again, people had said that kind of thing and nothing had ever happened.

"That night, when I was back at my house, I sat in my rocking chair on my back porch and looked across the valley over toward the village. I thought about starting the church and the school and was starting to formulate some plans. Suddenly, out of nowhere, I felt a choking sensation on my neck. Something was grabbing me, and I as sat there choking. I heard a voice saying, 'You will not build that church!'" As Willem described this, he gestured wildly with his hands at his neck and moved his shoulders back and forth as if he were choking while he steered the truck with his knees. "I said, 'In the name of Jesus, Get Out!' and immediately it was gone. I was completely still, and I just sat for a few moments." Willem paused for a moment then pointed his index finger straight ahead and continued with the same intensity, "Right then I headed out my door, ran all the way back down the mountain, through the river, and then up to the center of the village, where I had met with the elders. I was praying the whole time, talking to God about what had just happened. I marched right over to the ground where the church would be located and dedicated the church to God that very night."

Willem drove up the embankment and continued up the road. This road was completely different from the worn and broken concrete we were on before we crossed the river. This road was solid and smooth, with clean passage for water runoff on either side. Though the grade was quite steep, we were able to make progress quickly on it. While still primitive, the road was absolutely beautiful compared to the other country roads and paths in the area. When I interrupted his story and asked about the road, he simply replied, "This is our road. MTM built this." Willem continued his story as he drove. "We started the school first. The children in the village were put into classes, and we hired a couple of qualified teachers from Port-au-Prince. Right then and there, we formed the school. It was even before we had a single building." Willem laughed at the memory of the infant stages of the school.

He continued the story as he smoothly drove up the mountain. "That was in August of 1999. Then in October of the same year, we went to Indiana to incorporate Mountain Top Ministries (MTM). We put together a board of directors, filed the paperwork to become a 501(c)(3) organization, and began talking to people about the village, the school, and the church. We raised $7,000 and used that to build the first building for the school. We also

3

used the building for church on Sundays, as well as weekday evenings. Within a few months, Jesus became well known here. Over time, people gave their lives to Jesus Christ. The voodoo temples here on this mountain had their drums beating all night long. This place was owned by voodoo; every household practiced it. Now, all the voodoo priests are gone, and a church is here now. What a difference! At night, you don't hear the drums anymore."

The truck crested the top of the road and leveled off as we pulled in to the bustling village. Willem drove past two groups of students and a group of ladies sitting next to neatly organized baskets and selling food; he parked next to a basketball court. We exited the truck and took a few moments to look around at the numerous buildings that surrounded us.

"As you can see, that's the elementary school up there," Willem said pointing up the hill to a series of buildings cascading up the side of the mountain and surrounded by children. "We have fifteen classrooms, a cafeteria, library, a computer-training room, and a playground," he said as we saw kids climbing all over the monkey bars, teeter totters, and slides.

"The church is right here," Willem said pointing to a large, white square building that seated over 400 people. The prominent edifice boasts a massive steeple with a cross on the top, which was lit up like an airport every night, showing off the obvious Christian symbol on the top. "The voodoo drums don't beat any more at night, but everybody along this whole valley can see this steeple and the cross," Willem announced with a grin.

The trade school occupies the smaller twenty-by-forty-foot structure that used to be the church. "A few years ago, we built the larger church, and now the original church building is used for other things." Willem then directed our attention to the large building composed of a series of terraced classrooms, "This is the high school. We opened it two years ago and are still adding to it." The high school had a concrete reinforcing bar (rebar) pointing skyward from each corner and every weight-bearing pillar—a classic Haitian appearance of a building that was fully functioning but still under construction. The classrooms were full of students wearing clean blue uniforms.

"Over there, just past the water spigot, is the medical clinic. We have teams of American and Canadian doctors and nurses visit every month or so and provide the people with quality medical care. People come from all around the region to this village to see the doctors. Often, the crowd becomes so large that it's a real problem so we had to build another building just to serve as our waiting area, and it's this building over here." Willem pointed out each building as he described it. Then he motioned toward a large construction site just beyond the clinic and waiting room, "That area over there will be our future hospital." Willem continued, "Later on we'll take you to see the other school we operate in Dumay and also to see our children's home."

The buildings just seemed to keep on going and going. The vision for MTM was much more than a church and a school. We leaned back against the battered Chevy pickup and took it all in; none of this was here ten years ago. It's hard to believe that so much can happen in such a short time. I looked at Willem to ask a question, but he was already busy talking with two of his local leaders and dealing with pertinent issues of the day.

MTM began as a simple ministry of a church and a school in Haiti. It has grown and developed into far more than that and has touched the lives of thousands of Haitians and Americans alike. How did all of this happen? How did so much develop in a place with so little? MTM's story reveals God working through an amazingly resourceful man in a place with incredibly limited resources.

CHAPTER 2
EARLY DAYS

Lazy hands make a man poor, but diligent hands bring wealth.

Proverbs 10:4

Willem got up early to run down to the river and haul water for his family. His agile bare feet carried his slender, youthful body quickly down the hill. At the base of a magnificent tree with dark crawling vines were the constant voices of a hundred cicadas. The green canopy shielded the sun's fierce rays and created a cool chamber. The dusky water flowed into the five-gallon bucket as he submerged it. He paused to watch the neighbors head up the hill toward the road into the city. Some were heading to work but most were simply looking for a job. He strained as he carried the heavy load on top of his head all the way back up the hill to his home.

His father, a shoemaker, had passed away a few years earlier. Willem and his brother lived with their mother, grandmother, aunts, uncles, and cousins. A gas lamp sat in the center of a small wooden table of their ten-by-twenty-foot cinderblock one-room abode. Willem quietly placed the water on the dirt floor next to the table and sat down outside on a rock; he looked down the hill and over the rusted sheet metal roofs that covered the neighborhood of Thomassin forty.

On October 22, 1967, Willem's mother gave birth to a healthy boy right there in their home, with his grandmother in attendance. Since then, the humble home and surrounding neighborhood had been all he had known. Unlike many of his neighbors Willem had been privileged to attend school. His father provided for Willem's tuition all the way up to the sixth grade, but all that had changed after his father passed away.

Willem's mom was an excellent cook and managed to support the family by cooking for others out of her home. She cooked on a tight budget and relied on starchy foods like tubers, potatoes, and rice, making the food spicy with ti-malice (an onion-pepper relish) that added fire and flavor to everything, no matter how bland. Her specialties were *mayi moulen* (cornmeal mush flavored with peppers and coconut) and soup *jomou* (pumpkin soup). She also made good use of *djon-djon* (local black mushrooms), mixing them with rice for a satisfying meal. Willem sat patiently while irritated by flies; the majority of the meals went to the women carrying large baskets who came around mealtime and took the food away, leaving a few coins in payment. Food for the family came later, after the cooking for payment had been completed. Occasionally Willem's mother also sold various items at the local market to help earn enough to feed the family.

The meager wages she brought home provided for their food and clothing, but tuition was another matter entirely. Willem understood that if he were to have any further education, he would have to pay for it on his own. As he approached the seventh grade, he walked to the closest school available, which was a private school where the tuition was far beyond his reach. Disappointed, he went for a walk around the neighborhood, heading away from home. He certainly did not want to return there any time soon. His coal-black face held beads of sweat that turned to streams in the heat of the day. As he walked, he kicked a soup can back and forth between his bare feet with skilled soccer maneuvers.

He passed by the home of a white family and saw a boy a few years his junior in the yard kicking around a black-and-white soccer ball. He smiled and entered their yard. "Honor," he called out, a customary Haitian greeting a visitor uses to announce his or her presence when entering someone's domain.

"Respect," answered the blanc boy in Creole.

Willem introduced himself and asked if the boy wanted to play soccer.

"Sure," said the blanc. And after a couple of minutes playing in their yard, they headed down to the street and kept on playing. They played and talked for the rest of the day. Larry Neese Jr. was thirteen-years-old and the son of an American missionary. He and his family lived in a simple home just a short walk from Willem's family, and they were blessed with electricity as well as hot and cold running water.

At their first meeting, Willem managed to carry on a brief conversation with Larry's father (Larry Neese Sr.) despite his rudimentary English. Willem's first impression of Larry Sr. was that this was a tough, demanding man who held high expectations. Larry Sr. approved of his son's new friend and encouraged Willem to teach Larry Jr. better Creole.

Larry Jr. was an adventurous boy who wanted to go to and explore places that had never been discovered before. Together they explored every inch of the Thomassin area; one of their favorite areas was just a short walk away. It was a little flat area on the hill just across the riverbed from Thomassin forty-eight, and it became a center of their activities together when they stayed in town. Larry Jr. had a couple of extra dollars and was looking for some fun in this foreign land. Willem was a little older, had scoured the local landscape, and was anxious to go further and faster, but he lacked the resources. The two boys made a great pair. When Larry Jr. had a week off from school, he got his father to give them $20, and the two boys went exploring. They walked to the main road, Rue de Kenskoff, and headed for Port-au-Prince. They boarded a *tap-tap*, a brightly colored Toyota s-10 pickup truck with a roof on top and open sides. People can ride for a few cents, and dozens of people who don't seem to be bothered by personal space issues climb on board. Tap-taps are often overcrowded, with people spilling out the back and even standing on the bumper or sitting on the top. When the driver approaches the desired destination, the passenger taps on the cab window, and the driver stops for the passenger's exit. Thus the name tap-tap.

Larry Jr. flagged down the first tap-tap that he saw, but Willem refused to get on. In fact, he refused the first several tap-taps that came by. "I'm not going to sit in the back of one of these things like cattle," he said to his friend. So they waited for an empty one to come by. They flagged it down, and the two boys climbed in and sat in the front. So they made a practice of sitting in the front, and traveling comfortably wherever they liked.

"The Port of the Prince" the Haitian "Big Apple" was a great destination for adventure. The boys found the city to be a full of contrasts. This was a place where people were proud to live. Most of the secondary schools and virtually all of Haiti's universities and technical schools were there. Almost all public employees work there, and the vast majority of government expenditures are made there. This was the center of all political decisions, the commandments, and revolutions that have shaped Haitian history. The stoplights did not function, however, and police officers stood in the streets waving vehicles on and trying to enforce some semblance of order on the impatient, honking multitudes. Cracked, broken sidewalks and open sewers wait to sabotage the distracted driver or careless pedestrian. The streets were crammed with smoke-spewing trucks and muffler-free vehicles giving less than a car length between vehicles as they wound around the pothole-filled roads.

The boys quickly got their fill of the city. They saw the sights, ate leisurely, and headed for the bus station to seek adventure at the coast. The bus station was an unpaved muddy lot. Two-cylinder motorbikes scurried around them as they walked past piles of foul-smelling garbage that swarmed with flies. Street vendors peddled unwrapped bread, fabric, sugarcane, colorful dresses, shirts, sandals, pots and pans, and cola. The buses were large, brightly colored Mack flatbed trucks secondarily equipped with benches and rickety vertical sides. The roofs were overloaded with baskets and trunks heading for the market.

Willem and Larry Jr. boarded a bus labeled God is Great, which they had heard was headed for a small, quiet coastal town. After a bumpy ride with chickens and goats on board with them, they arrived at Leogane. They spent a few days exploring and enjoying the beach. Larry Jr. went swimming, scuba diving, and fishing while Willem struck up conversations with people on the shore. He had a knack of making friends quickly and got to know people everywhere he went. He not only met people but also would spend time with them, find out what they did, where they worked, and what their family was like. Then, he remembered the name of every person he met and looked forward to coming back for another visit. Their exploration was complete with restaurants and hotels or sometimes they stayed overnight in the homes of their new friends. A long bus ride home yielded numerous stories for family and friends back home, and the two boys bonded as brothers.

"One day his father came up to me," Willem recalled, "He said, 'Willem, you are teaching Larry Jr. Creole and that's good, but I want you to know that some day he will leave this country. You need to push him to also teach you English.' I was shocked, I had not thought that my friend would ever leave." Larry Jr. was the first person to spend any time speaking English with Willem. They went to work right away. Within a few weeks he was making major strides, and after about a year, he was fluent.

Salvation

Willem recalled, "When I was about fifteen-years-old Larry Jr. and I did everything together. He invited me to come to one of the conferences that his father was having. So I went there, and it was some nice stuff—something that I had never heard before." This was not a crusade or evangelistic meeting, but a pastors training seminar. Willem continued, "That was the first time I had ever heard about Jesus. I had seen churches around but never gone inside, and the next thing you know I was sitting around a bunch of pastors and big stuff, you know. I decided to go forward and accept Christ, but they did not have an altar call because everyone there was a pastor. Later that day, I talked to the pastor and told him that I wanted to accept Christ, and he was really happy."

Larry Sr. walked Willem through the gospel message and together they prayed, "God, I know that I have broken your laws, and my sin has separated me from you. I believe that your son, Jesus Christ, died for my sins, was resurrected from the dead, and is alive today. I invite Jesus in to take charge of my life. I am truly sorry, and now I want to turn away from my sinful life and turn toward you. Please forgive me, and help me avoid sinning again. In Jesus' name I pray. Amen."

At that point, Willem's life changed dramatically. He said, "The next thing I know I was there the next day with my notebook and my Bible taking notes. And three months later I was up front translating for pastors."

Willem began working for Larry Sr. doing odd jobs. He started by running simple errands for him and doing more as trust was built. This was his first job for pay. Between working for Larry Sr. and hanging out with Larry Jr., Willem was thoroughly enveloped in the world of a Christian family. Larry Sr. was the only example of a Christian man and role model that Willem had so he watched his every move.

He remembered, "I saw firsthand singing Christian music and saw people pray at the table before they eat—good Christian stuff in the home. He really helped me move forward. I learned by watching Larry Sr. live his life. I watched everything he did, and I learned from him. I was also interpreting for him from the pulpit every Sunday. Larry Sr. was a very tough guy."

One day, Larry Sr. was giving Willem a ride in his car, and Willem wrote the name Jesus on the door inside the car with a pencil. Larry Sr. was furious and sought out Willem and yelled, "Who wrote this?"

Willem admitted to the vandalism but didn't see the error in his ways since he was simply writing his savior's name on the car. But Larry Sr. was harsh with him and said, "Don't you ever write on my car or anyone else's car any more."

Willem remembers, "I thought, 'This guy is a missionary?' I wrote something about Jesus, and I didn't think that would be a problem." While the issue was small, the inconsistency between sharing love gently from the pulpit and firmly from the hand was obvious. And Willem learned an early lesson in working with people, "He got so upset I realized that in life you don't invade people's property like that."

Willem continued to drink from the faucet of spiritual understanding from the unique position as the interpreter in Larry Sr.'s pulpit. Often guest preachers would come for a few days or weeks and Willem would interpret for them also. They would open the scriptures and pour out messages of all kinds for the people. Willem interpreted simple messages of the gospel, complex messages of wine and new wineskins, and everything in between.

Willem also became familiar with scripture as well, reading and studying on his own. His biblical training came primarly from being the conduit for missionaries. While he never took a class in preaching technique, he experienced it firsthand as he was the voice through whom his peers learned God's word.

With the money he saved from his job, Willem enrolled in seventh grade and continued his education. Generously, Larry Sr. purchased the school uniforms Willem was required to wear. They did not have off-the-rack shirts and pants, so the custom was to have the uniforms made by a local tailor. This was not because they wanted custom-made, fancy outfits; rather it was an affordable way to have the students all wear matching uniforms. Larry Sr. gave Willem the money, and he purchased the fabric and went to get measured by the tailor. Willem insisted on a Henley collar, which was different from the traditional collar that all the other students at the school had. He gave the tailor specific directions for the type and look of his shirt. He wanted to look sharp and be set apart from his classmates.

Over the next couple of years, Larry Jr. and Willem attended the same school and were inseparable. Often, a large, black limousine, part of an official motorcade, would stop and the passenger would roll down the window and offer the boys a ride to school. The considerate passenger, and the reason for the official motorcade, was none other than Jean Claude "Baby Doc" Duvalier, the undisputed strongman and president of the country who ruled with an iron fist. "He couldn't have been nicer," Larry Jr. recalled. "Any time he saw us walking to school, he would stop and offer us a ride. I only learned much later in life about the many terrible things he had done."

The boys' exploits became more mature when Larry Jr. acquired a car. Then they were able to take off more frequently and go farther with more autonomy. They drove through the fertile and misty heights of the mountain ranges, down in the desert scrub, through dry, rutted roads, and to the coast. They traveled sandy roads overlooking the Canal de Saint-Marc and got familiar with National Highway Route One, the principal highway that bisects the country. Everywhere they went, Willem spoke with people at length and made friends in every town and village.

They drove along pitted roads and through choking clouds of dust as they dodged traffic, cattle, goats, and boulders. The skeletons of sidelined buses and cars made for unique scenery as they passed through green patchwork of rice paddies near the decaying port town of Montrouls and beside the beautiful aqua sea. They stayed overnight, and together they explored the cliffs and caves along the coast and caught all types of critters and snakes. In their teenage energy Willem and Larry Jr. saw and experienced all types of adventure.

Willem's Room

Larry Jr. couldn't spend time at Willem's house because there simply wasn't enough space for them. They ran all around the neighborhood and spent a lot of time at the Neese's home. After Larry Sr. paid a visit to Willem's home, he decided to come to the aid of the young Haitian. He bought several bags of cement and a small truckload of sand. They used a block mold, and went to work mixing and pouring their own cement blocks. After the blocks dried, Larry Sr. worked with the help of the boys to level out a foundation and built three ten-foot cinderblock walls on the back of Willem's family's home, creating a separate room for Willem. They fabricated a door and roof from sheet metal and left the window space open. The two boys then had their own private space to hang out. At night, they slept on cardboard or straw mats over the dirt floor.

When they weren't out exploring, the two boys were right there in Willem's new room. It didn't take long for them to start wondering how to get some of the modern conveniences that Larry Jr. had in his home over in Willem's room. Larry Sr. bought a very basic light fixture and a small radio for Willem, but there was no power source. As the two boys sat outside the house with their backs against the sun-warmed cinderblock wall, they looked up and beyond the moths that flew sporadically over their heads, and saw black wires zigzagging above the neighborhood. These electric wires were suspended by telephone poles, which were interspersed in a seemingly random fashion. They looked down the road and just two houses down was a telephone pole holding countless wires. It was amazing that the wires stayed in place with the haphazard arrangement on the solitary pole.

After thinking and planning for a few days, the adventurous boys climbed a nearby telephone pole. Using wire cutters, they exposed a pair of wires and then connected an extension cord. They taped the connection and ran their wire along with a couple of other wires to the location where the wires crossed over Willem's house; they rigged it so the wire descended right through Willem's window. Suddenly, they had power for a functioning light and radio right there in his room. Pictures of Porsches and BMWs that he got from magazines covered every inch of the room like wallpaper. In comparison to living with a dozen men women and children as he had before, Willem now had a very comfortable home!

Willem's mom continued to cook meals of red beans, cornmeal, and yams under clouds of smoke spewed by stoves fueled by dried twigs and charcoal. Occasionally Larry Jr. was able to convince his father to part with five dollars for a special treat. They gave the money to Willem's mom who went to the local market and came back with a full-grown purring cat. She killed it and cooked the cat for the boys, which they enjoyed with great delight. Larry Jr. recalled, "Willem's mom made the best cat on the island."

Real Estate

Willem continued to work for Larry Sr. and also got the opportunity to interpret for several other missionaries in the region. In Haiti, there are missionaries coming and going all the time. The poverty-stricken country receives help from foreign agencies, governments, churches, and even individuals. It was common to see a pickup truck driving by with eight or ten white people huddled in the back on the way to one of the various mission organizations. Many of them come for only a week or so, but a large number come for six months or even a year or two. These people all needed places to stay. Willem recalled, "As I got to know them, I saw these missionaries looking for homes right here around Thomassin. If they were planning on staying for any length of time, they would need to rent a home. So I started looking for homes for them, and when I found them a home that they liked, they would give me a commission." So Willem started talking to real estate agents, just asking around to find out who would be moving and where there were available homes. "The next thing I knew, I would find the owner and ask if he wanted the house rented out. If he did, I would bring my clients in, and when they rented the place, I got a commission. It was a very good start for me."

Word spread quickly and new missionaries who came for the first time were told to contact Willem when they arrived so that he could help them get settled. "Later on," Willem continued, "once I got my car, I offered something different nobody else offered. I would go visit the missionary, sit down and talk to him, and he would tell me exactly what he was looking for in a house and how much he was willing to spend. Then I took him in my car to go look at a few houses, and I would try to match the missionaries with what they were looking for. They didn't have to pay for gas or anything if they didn't like the house. But I would usually find them the right house because I knew what was available at the time." Willem continued, "At one time I had placed every missionary from Petionville all the way to Kenscoff in their homes."

These missionaries then continued to rely on Willem as a local resource while they were there. Various mission organizations from the local mountainous area, some from down in Port-au-Prince and others far away used him to help with translating. "I translated for them all the time," Willem said. "For crusades, for individual counseling, for Bible studies—anything they needed. And I would not receive a dime. God blessed me, and I wanted to do something for the kingdom, so I helped by translating." After several years of experience with a variety of different American speakers and styles, Willem became one of the best translators in the country.

Soccer

Another area in which Willem excelled was Haiti's only organized sport, soccer. "I played soccer ever since I could walk," he said. They would play with an avocado seed as a ball. (Avocado seeds can grow up to the size of baseballs in Haiti). "We would use a carnation milk can and kick that around when we didn't have a ball. We were barefooted whether it was flat or hilly. We just played."

When he was seven-years-old, Willem was signed up on his first organized team. The team got together with a coach and learned the basics of the game. They didn't have uniforms or any fancy equipment; they just got together two teams that were shirts and skins. He managed to be involved with organized soccer throughout his childhood. By the time he got to high school, he had plenty of experience and tried out for the high school team. He not only made the team, but his leadership potential showed. He explained, "I was team captain, but that doesn't mean you were the best player. I think the team captain is the guy who is well-disciplined. It meant that he was a leader." Soccer was more than a fun game for Willem—it was an education in leadership. He normally played midfielder and coordinated play on the field. The investment he paid on the fields through sweat and tears paid dividends later.

The team traveled to play against other high schools, and over the course of the season, the kids talked about their heroes on the national team. And they dreamed of being among the best in the country. In 1989, after the high school season was over, Willem decided to see what was possible and showed up to the Haiti National Team tryouts. After a week of strenuous workouts, Willem was rewarded with a spot on the team.

Having accomplished his goal, Willem was at an all time high. The country however was in a severe depression, and the unemployment level was skyrocketing. The government managed to continue to support the team but was unable to give the players much financially. They practiced every day and were given shoes and new uniforms. Willem remembered, "We played soccer with guys that didn't have money to take a tap-tap home. Many of the guys on the team were getting by on just one meal a day, and they didn't pay us anything. So there wasn't much encouragement there. People want to be on the national team, and you have your name that you made it there, but that's it."

After working out as a team for a few months, they had the opportunity to represent their country and play against other national teams. The cost of airline tickets and hotel accommodations prohibited their travel to other countries. Haiti did, however host other national teams in rivaled competition. During his time on the team, they hosted teams including Jamaica and Suriname (a small South American country).

Willem was disillusioned by the whole experience. "When you've been there, you feel that you've not accomplished anything. You know, we had practice a lot, and that was a big deal. But we didn't have a good coach at the time, and for me, there never was much to talk about. Playing soccer is not just about what you do on the field. It's more involved than that. Looking at my life, I couldn't see where I was going with this. I had so much to do other than playing that game. I love to play soccer, and I still play every week, but that is not what I'm about."

Willem remembered, "There was a guy on our team who was a great player. He carried our team on his shoulders and was a very good guy. But he would be asking people for money to buy food, and we'd give him three bucks to buy lunch. He was the best player on the team but didn't even make it outside the lines of the soccer field. A guy like that could coach little kids, and he could do a lot of things using his soccer skills. The opportunity had never been given to him. I'm not going to say that he never went out and tried. It's just that that opportunity didn't materialize. People can know me for years and not even know that I was on Haiti's national team because I never mention it to anybody. I guess the bottom line was that being on the team alone isn't accomplishing anything."

Cars

Larry Jr. left Haiti and moved back to the States just as his father had predicted. Willem quickly realized that things would be different without his buddy's vehicle to get around in. Willem found a car for sale for only $900; it needed some small repairs but was basically in good shape, so he bought it. He parked it in the alley near his home, and every day after school, he went to work fixing it up. He acquired some tools, and after a few simple repairs, he turned around and sold the car for $1,800. "That was a great feeling," he said.

Larry Jr. said, "Willem called me, and told me about the car and said that he could make good money doing this."

Willem used the profits to purchase another car that he fixed up and drove around for a few months before selling. He was still a teenager and attending high school at the time. "A lot of teachers in my school didn't have cars. They took a tap-tap to school every day. Some of the principals didn't even have a car. But here was this high school student who was driving a car to school every day. You know, it was great." Over the next several years, Willem was continually in the process of buying, fixing, and selling cars. When he saw one for sale that looked like it was underpriced or could be fixed, he bought it. When somebody made an offer on a car that he had, he sold it. When missionaries needed a car, he was there to help with that, too. His house always had a couple of cars around in various stages of repair and resale; it's a tradition he has kept up to this day (although rarely does he sell cars but uses them at MTM).

In 1991, one of Willem's friends was dating a young man named Mark. Willem got to know Mark and found out that he worked in the U.S. embassy. They became friends, and Mark invited him down to the embassy to play basketball. A natural athlete, Willem took to the game quickly and learned to dribble and pass during the warm-up for his first pick-up game. His jump shot took a little longer to master, but in the process, he got some coaching from some of the guys at the embassy.

As he walked through the embassy parking lot on his way to play basketball one day, he noticed a young man climbing out of a BMW. Willem stopped and admired the car. He said, "Man, I want to buy that BMW."

The young man said, "How much do you want to pay?"

Willem replied with a laugh, "I'll give you $5,000." As a car aficionado, he knew the car's worth was over $20,000.

A few months later Willem received a phone call. The man on the other line did not identify himself but simply said, "Do you have the money?"

Willem inquired, "What for?"

He said, "To buy my BMW that you like so much."

Willem said, "I thought you were joking."

He replied, "If you want to buy the car, I need the money today because I'm leaving the country tomorrow."

Willem emptied his bank account and came up with the money. He went down to the embassy and stopped when he saw the BMW in the parking lot. He smiled as he admired the silver blue, shiny sedan. After finding the owner and having a brief discussion, Willem handed over the money, signed the title paper, and received the keys. The next day, the previous owner was out of the country.

Willem recalled, "That day I became the coolest guy in the country, driving my new BMW! I drove that car for a couple of years and then sold it for $20,000."

School

Willem attended school through tenth grade at the French school not far from his home; then he went to an American high school in Petionville. When he became busy with all his other jobs, he decided to hold off on school. "School wasn't for me." He said, "I was just an average kid at school and was doing so many other things." Continuing to translate and work for missionaries, running his real estate business, and dealing in cars kept him constantly busy. "School in Haiti was all memorizing, just regurgitating what the teacher said. But I was working and doing well." So he stopped attending school for a couple of years and spent most of his time working.

"But the Americans I worked for kept insisting that education was the key for success. And they were right." Willem continued working while he pursued a GED, a monumental task for most Haitians; he achieved that goal at the age of twenty-one. Willem's real opportunities came through his knowledge of the English language. This opened many doors for him in the world between Haiti and the United States. Willem said, "I give God the credit for who I am today. God has blessed me and brought many opportunities."

Scandal

When Willem was nineteen years old, he met a missionary family who had brought along their seventeen-year-old daughter who was actively involved in the missionary work. It didn't take long for Willem to take notice of her. They began spending a lot of time together and began dating. Willem said, "After a while we thought we loved each other and thought we would get married. We were crazy. But the family did not respect our relationship."

Her mom said to Willem, "I don't want you for my daughter because you are black." She said, "You are a great man, and I believe you are going to go far in life because you have a lot going for you."

Willem chuckled as he remembered the conversation, "She was prophesying, you know!"

She said, "The one problem I have with you is that you are black. I don't want you for my daughter."

So without the blessing of the family, they were at a crossroads. Willem said, "We decided that if we had a baby, it would force them to marry us. And then we can go on with our lives." A couple of months later while she was on vacation back in the States, the girl found out that she was pregnant. She was going to have the baby right before she turned eighteen. Her family responded quickly and made arrangements for her to give the baby up for adoption.

Willem found out about this through the mail. "She sent me a letter that said she was going to give the baby up for adoption. I had no say and no power in the situation.

It was a closed adoption. The adoptive parents don't know who the original parents were, and the original parents have no way to find the baby." After that letter, she made no further contact with Willem and didn't respond to his subsequent letters and calls.

Willem said, "I thought I knew it all. I thought I had a good reason, but that does not give me the right to get pregnant before marriage, biblically." Nothing disrupts a church or missionary community like a sex scandal, and Willem was right in the middle of a number of missionary organizations.

He said, "I had a missionary friend who was like a mother to me, and she told me, 'Son, it takes two to tango. You have to recognize what you did was wrong. You need to repent, and God will honor that. The only way for you to be blessed—yes, the *only* way—is for you to recognize with your whole heart that you were wrong. And one day, if you have a chance, you go to the girl's family and tell them you were wrong. Go straight to the girl and tell her you were wrong, and God will bless you.'"

Willem thought about that advice for quite a while. "That's when I got down on my knees, nineteen-years ago, and I cried. I told God, 'I was wrong.'" The first step of repentance was complete. His heart was right, he had learned some lessons, but the child was still out there, and this would affect any future relationship he would have.

"That was something I had to live with in my life for a long time. I remember that I said, a long time ago, 'In the name of Jesus I will find this baby some day.' I was confident that I had God's promise that I will find this child some day."

A couple of years later, Willem fell in love with a young lady named Beth Tyron who he met when she visited for a couple of weeks with a mission team. When Willem started to develop a relationship with Beth, he was quick to tell her about the whole issue. Beth listened to Willem, looked at him, and said, "You were really stupid." They knew that this would be something they would deal with for the rest of their lives. Surrounded by missionaries in his daily life, Willem sought out godly wisdom, received it, and put it into action. Just after they were married, a pastor suggested that they find the girl's parents and apologize.

Willem and Beth and their pastor all met with the girl's family at a nearby restaurant. Willem said to this family, "I know this is not what you wanted for your daughter. You wanted her to go to school and finish college, but I went ahead and got your daughter pregnant. And I want you to know that I'm sorry for what I did. And if you've ever said anything unkind to me, I forgive you. And I want you to forgive me for what I've done, as well."

The mother looked straight in his face and blatantly told him, "There is nothing you can say, and there is nothing you can do that will enable me to forgive you." That was pretty much the end of the conversation. As hurtful as the words were, Willem had still done his part. That enabled him to go on in life with his wife's blessing.

All of these years, these things weighed on Willem's heart. He found out about ways to find adopted children. With the Internet it's easier than ever to find adopted kids. Adopted children commonly look for their mothers, and once that quest is successful, they start looking for their fathers. Willem had been trying to make contact for many years. Once the child was over the age of eighteen, Willem went online to an adoptive family site and entered their demographic information. They included the child's birthday, their names, and the area in Haiti they lived and worked as missionaries. With this information it should be easy to put Willem together with his child.

It didn't take long for Willem's old girlfriend to see what he was doing on line. "The family got really upset, and she sent me an e-mail and my old girlfriend said, 'If you clean up your mess from the Internet, I'll talk to you.'"

"I said, 'Oh, that's what I've been after for the last nineteen years. So she finally talked to me.' My old girlfriend's mother realized that we were so close to finding her that she panicked about me possibly finding her first. As it turns out, she had been checking on me all the time on the Internet. She knew about MTM, and she had seen how God has used me. She cried just like a baby. And I asked her for her forgiveness. We set up a time for her, my whole family, and me to be on the phone and on the Internet at the same time. We all were excited. She shared with us a picture of my daughter. Finally after nineteen years I know that I have a daughter. After nineteen years, I had never known if the baby was a boy or a girl. But I finally found out about my daughter."

Willem and Beth have discussed the whole issue openly with their two boys. Beth concluded, "There has been a pattern in Willem's life that when he seeks out godly wisdom, he applies it, and puts feet to the words. I think God has honored that. Willem may be stubborn up to that point, but he will eventually come to a place where his level of pride will drop, and he will humble himself and do what he knows needs to be done."

CHAPTER 3
HAITIAN BEGINNINGS

Vindicate me, O God, and plead my cause against an ungodly nation;
rescue me from deceitful and wicked men.

Psalm 43:1

The island of Hispaniola is about the size of South Carolina and is remarkable for it's contrasts. The Republic of Haiti, the poorest country in the Western Hemisphere, occupies the western third of the island, and the remainder of the island is the Dominican Republic, a popular vacation destination. When people visit this Caribbean island, only 600 miles from Miami, the contrast is easily seen. Most people ask some version of the same questions: "How did Haiti get to be like this?" Or the more intriguing, "When two countries are on the same island, why is one a beautiful tropical paradise, and the other such a mess?" Then people ask, "What does Haiti need to do to improve her situation?" In order to get a grip on these questions and understand how Haiti became one of the poorest countries in the world, we have to take a look at its history.

Willem took me to visit the National History Museum in Port-au-Prince. We parked about a half block from the presidential palace, and he pointed out a round, white building built low into the ground just to the left of the palace. We descended the concrete steps from the sidewalk and opened the door. The nicely air-conditioned building was empty except a couple of guards and a young lady at the small desk near the door. Willem engaged her in a conversation for a few minutes, gave her a few Haitian bills, and we entered the museum. Just past a round twenty-foot white marble structure in the center of the building were four life-size bronze busts. Willem introduced them to me as the founding fathers of the country, explaining that all four of these men were buried right in the center of the building. This was not only a historical museum but also a mausoleum commemorating Haiti's founding fathers. The building was literally built around their remains.

The gravesite was flanked by the national coat of arms carved in wood and plated in gold. There was a central palm tree flanked by guns, flags, a drum, cannon balls, and two cannon. Assuming that the structure was rich in symbolism, I asked Willem what the flags and cannon represented. He had a curious look on his face and turned to find a professional guide who worked in the building full time. When the guide came over, we introduced ourselves, and I repeated my question to him. He said that he did not know but went on to explain that underneath the coat of arms sat the actual remains of Jean-Jacques Dessalines, Alexandre Pétion and Henri Christophe. However since Toussaint Louverture died in a prison in France, his symbolic remains (dirt from the French prison) are buried alongside his colleagues.

Discovery

Our tour officially started when our guide took us on a stroll through the artifacts of the Taino Indians. The five Taino kingdoms are well represented in the museum with their art and early artifacts. When Christopher Columbus sailed the ocean blue with his three ships, he made his first landing on the island of Hispaniola in 1492. He landed in the Northern Taino Kingdom, land that is now the Republic of Haiti. The Tainos had developed a flourishing civilization long before Columbus's voyage to the Americas. The museum proudly displays the eight-foot tall original anchor from the *Santa Maria*.

Attracted by the gold on the island, the Spanish occupied Haiti and renamed it Hispaniola, which means little Spain. Over a million Tainos occupied the island when the Spanish first arrived.

But with their advanced weaponry and desire for conquest, the Spanish quickly conquered the natives and reduced them to slavery. Fifty years later, most of the Tainos in Haiti were wiped out either through the hardship of their condition as slaves or from diseases they contracted from the Spaniards. The genocide of the Tainos in Haiti was brutal, and the annihilation of the Taino Indians was one of the most complete in history.

Our guide took us a few feet past the Taino display and showed us display of early French artifacts. In 1625, French adventurers settled on the island, and in spite of the Spanish occupation, they saw the prosperous tropical island as a potential French colony. After many years of struggling for power, in 1697 Spain and France signed the Treaty of Ryswick, which allowed Spain to control eastern two-thirds, which became the Dominican Republic and ceded the remainder to France. That portion, about the size of Maryland would become Haiti. Our guide laid out this process by showing large maps on the walls that outlined the previous five Taino Kingdoms, and the new French and Spanish territories.

The French operated flourishing plantations in the fertile tropical soil and imported thousands of slaves from Africa to do the heavy lifting. The guide reported that over thirteen million slaves left Africa en route to the island, but in the process of transporting the chained prisoners across the ocean, more than two million died. Those who survived arrived emaciated and weak from the weeks or months of starvation in transit. Over the course of the next few decades, the French plantations flourished and the island became immensely profitable. On the backs of the slaves, the French developed their third of the island into the single richest colony in the world! The importation of the black slaves in large numbers forever changed the demographic face Haiti.

Willem turned toward me and explained the roots of Haiti's class struggle, "To understand the racial divide, you need to know your history. When a French man saw a nice-looking slave woman, he went and slept with her. And they would have a baby, a mulatto with nice hair and nice skin just like my son. That French man says, 'My son is going to have an education.' So the mulatto people had the privileges of the white men and were not slaves. But people with dark skin had no rights and got no education."

A fifty-pound ball sat next to a three-foot-long curved piece of wood on the floor in front of Willem's feet. "This is how they would punish runaway slaves," our guide told us. "They would tie this wooden yoke around the slave's neck and chain his hands and feet to it then connect it to the weight." Slaves were kept in bondage for extended periods of time dragging the weight everywhere they went. The plantation owners were merciless on a day-to-day basis, and disobedience was punished with severe beatings or even execution.

The Africans who now occupied this island in mass numbers brought over not only their muscles, which were to do the work on the plantation but their entire culture, including their language and religion. Living primarily in huts with one another, they spoke their native African tongue. But by necessity they learned the French terminology from their new bosses. What resulted is a distinct language called Haitian Creole, and while the vocabulary is mostly of French origin, it also has strong characteristics of African languages. This has remained the language of the people to this day. Missionaries first developed Haitian Creole as a written language in the 1940s and translated the Bible into Haitian Creole. But it wasn't until 1979 that this written system was given any recognition. French is the language of business and is what is taught primarily in schools, and other than the Bible, there are few books in Creole. French is the national language and all the governmental documents (birth certificates, driver's licenses, etc.) and anything of importance are in French.

The capture and redistribution of individuals sold into slavery fragmented families from various tribes and countries. Out of necessity they pooled their religious knowledge and became culturally unified both with their language and religion. The religious leaders included the various spirits and entities of many different African nations and formed a religion that they practiced wholeheartedly that is now known as Haitian voodoo. The French plantation owners were largely Catholic and insisted on their slaves becoming Christians. The slaves would attend mass and dutifully recite the Roman Catholic liturgy. Rather than resist the indoctrination, the slaves incorporated various elements of Catholicism into their own religious practice. They managed to maintain their own worship of voodoo spirits even right under the noses of their masters during mass. Today, voodoo temples are filled with icons of Catholic saints that represent various voodoo spirits.

Willem explained this whole process, concluding, "As a result, Catholicism has a different meaning to the people here in Haiti. In some ways it is synonymous with voodoo, which has taken many symbols from the Catholic Church and used them to represent their spirits. How crafty of Satan. Now, if you see a statue of the Virgin Mary, you have to wonder is it Catholic or representative of some voodoo god?"

The Haitian Revolution

In 1787, the resounding message from the French Revolution was Liberty, Equality, and Fraternity. The tight ties between France and Haiti ensured that everything happening in France became well-known throughout its most profitable colony. The population of the colony comprised blacks, mulattoes, and a small minority of whites. The mulattoes claimed to be political equal with the whites, but the whites were busy demanding from France the right to participate in the running of the colony that they occupied and ruled. The blacks however were treated as harshly as any slave community in history. These three groups were set against one another across a deep racial divide. This happened to be during the same period as the class struggle in France, which became the French Revolution.

The slaves heard the message of the French Revolution and knew that the concepts of Liberty, Equality, and Fraternity were far from the reality that they experienced from their brutal slave owners. As the slaves' contention began to boil over, they invented their own form of protest. The museum guide showed me a list of names in bronze letters across the top of a wall. "These are the freedom fighters," he said. "The runaway slaves would hide in the mountains and come down at night and kill their slave masters." I recognized the name Mackanda as the most famous of them all and pointed to it.

"Yes," he said. "François Mackanda was a voodoo priest who escaped from the plantation where he was a slave and hid in the mountains." Our guide explained that he formed a militia with a band of escaped slaves. From their retreat, they came down at night to poison or kill their masters. He continued this rebellion for six years, and his following grew as the hope of equality gained a foothold in the minds of the slave population. During this time, Mackanda and his followers poisoned and killed as many as 6,000 whites. Eventually, he was caught and executed in the public square of Cap Haitian.

Then I pointed to Boukman, another bronzed name on the wall. Once again, our guide smiled and told the story. On August 14, 1791, Boukman, a voodoo priest, held a meeting in the northern mountains of the island for the slaves to voice their hatred of the white men. The meeting was in the form of a voodoo ceremony. As the runaway slaves voiced their resentment of their deplorable conditions, rum flowed freely, traditional voodoo drums beat out the rhythm, and they danced around a bonfire. The sky was raging with clouds and rain soaked them to the skin, when a woman started dancing wildly through the crowd. With a knife in her hand, she cut the throat of a pig and collected the blood, which she distributed to everyone present. They made a vow to kill all the white people on the island and sealed the promise by drinking the blood in the traditional voodoo manner. Willem gave the grave conclusion to the story, "This sacrifice was officially not only the beginning of the rebellion, but the ceremony in which the country was dedicated to voodoo."

At that point, the blacks began a full-fledged warfare on the whites. They killed every white man, woman, and child they met and set the plantations on fire. The French army fought back, and captured and killed Boukman. However, the ideas of Liberty, Equality, Fraternity were firmly planted in the mind of the slaves, and Boukman became a martyr for the rebellion. The Revolution that would give birth to the Republic of Haiti had begun, and nothing could stop it.

As we continued to make our way slowly through the halls of history, our guide pointed out an ancient looking three-foot-high bronze bell. "This is the Haitian Liberty Bell," he said. They rang the bell proclaiming, Live free or die. We saw the portrait of Toussaint Louverture, a former slave who emerged as a leader during the revolt. Our guide said, "Toussaint became known as the father of the nation of Haiti." He proved to be a military genius, and he configured the masses of the slaves into a well-organized army. With political manipulation and military campaigns, he gained notoriety in the colony. From 1791 to 1800, Toussaint manipulated the French and Spaniards into fighting against one another. He managed to eliminate all his enemies until he was the only power left on the island. Toussaint was arrested and imprisoned in the French Alps where he died, but one of his generals Jean-Jacques Dessalines rose up and said, "You killed the trunk, but the tree will continue to grow." And Dessalines continued the struggle with France.

Later that day, we drove through Port-au-Prince and past a statue of Dessalines on a horse in battle uniform with his sword drawn. Willem's friend Rachael Denache McIntosh recounted a slightly different version of the story. Looking up at the statue, with a smile on her face, she said that she remembered as a young girl learning in school that Dessalines rallied the slave army in a mighty battle. He rode his horse straight at the French army with bullets coming, charged ahead with his sword drawn, and yelled, "Let's go!" The French respected him so much for his bravery that they forfeited the battle.

"When I was a kid," Willem said to me. "I didn't play cowboys and Indians like you probably did. In the schoolyard, we played out the roles of Toussaint and Dessalines, our heroes from the Haitian Revolution." They battled until January 1, 1804, when Haiti emerged as the first black independent republic. The heroes of the independence celebrated their victory for weeks at the plantations that they had burned in the process of the war.

The victorious former slaves were now free, and they celebrated with food that had been previously forbidden to slaves and had grand meal of pumpkin soup. Many years later, pumpkin soup remains a traditional symbol of freedom and drinking the soup is a celebration much like the American turkey at the Thanksgiving table.

Jean-Jacques Dessalines renamed the country using its original Taino name, Haiti, to honor the memory of the Indians who had been massacred by the Spanish. He became Haiti's first president, and he set out to complete his personal ambition of freeing the country from any white domination. He made sure that they completely eliminated the possibility of a return to French authority over them. Our guide showed us one of the original Haitian flags and explained that France's tricolor flag with its vertical strips of red, white, and blue influenced Dessalines. He took the blue to symbolize the blacks, the red for the mulattoes and ripped out the white stripe from the middle declaring that Haiti would be free from the domination of white men! He oriented the stripes horizontally and made a new Haitian two-color flag. (The coat of arms, drawn by Pétion, was added to the flag in 1843.) Dessalines went on a warpath and made good on his promise to eliminate the remaining white men. He killed 3,200 Frenchmen in the island's second genocide and declared, "We have repaid these cannibals—war for war, crime for crime, outrage for outrage."

Willem explained, "He ordered the killing of all Frenchmen remaining on the island. But some of these French men were part Haitian, mulattoes, so they couldn't kill them. They were the educated ones, and they ruled the country. Ever since then, they have been the problem." The whites were eliminated, the mulattoes became the new elite of Haiti, and the class struggle continued.

The island's second genocide resulted in an international embargo against the infant country. Internationally, the country was ostracized; Haiti had no diplomatic relations with any nations in Europe or the United States. The French government refused to recognize the republic as an independent state and later required the payment of 150 million francs as indemnity from the new nation.

"At this point," Willem said. "The colony that had been rich with flourishing plantations, sat in ruins with burned plantations. The leaders with any formal education and experience in running plantations had been killed." Dessalines ruled with his contemporaries, Alexandre Pétion, and Henri Christophe, but after only two years, they had an insurrection among them. Pétion and Christophe assassinated Dessalines while he was entering Port-au-Prince on October 17, 1806. This marked the first of many bloody takeovers in Haitian history.

After the president's death, the country had several short presidencies until Jean Pierre Boyer took control in 1820 in another violent succession. Boyer considered France's refusal to recognize the new nation as an independent country to be the worst threat to Haiti's integrity. The fledgling country needed to trade to be successful, and he saw paying off the French as the only means of making that happen. In 1825, he agreed to pay 150 million francs to France; however, at the time Haiti did not have that amount in their government coffers. Therefore Boyer not only emptied the treasury but also mortgaged the country's future to the French. So the nation was recognized and free to conduct trade, but was completely destitute and without strong leadership.

The Duvalier Dynasty

We stood by a wall with two rows of neatly arranged photographs of every Haitian president since Dessalines. Our guide pointed out that some preferred to be called emperor, dictator, or king, but they all held the same office, and they were in danger of their own army if people were unhappy. Of the twenty-two heads of state between 1843 and 1915 one was blown up with his palace, one was poisoned, one was hacked to pieces by a mob, three died while serving, and one resigned. The army deposed the other fourteen in revolution, and only one served out his presidential term in office. Some were in power temporarily as the court ruled between deposed leaders and the next election; some were in power for a few months or years before being ousted, overruled, or assassinated.

As we walked slowly down the wall of leaders, Willem jumped down the line to the photograph of Dr. François Duvalier. He said, "When Duvalier was in charge, there was a sense of leadership in the country. You knew who was in charge." He explained that Duvalier was a black doctor who went all over the mountains treating people for no charge. Early in his career, he made connections all over the country and became very popular among the common people; he became known as Papa Doc. He won acclaim for helping the poor fight malaria other tropical diseases that ravaged Haiti for years. He also managed to have girlfriends in towns all over the country but never had any children with any of them. He was loved by the people and won the election of 1957.

Papa Doc also worked quickly to secure his position of authority. Our guide ran his hand along the wall of presidents who preceded Duvalier and said, "Papa Doc knew what happened to these other men, so he rewrote the constitution to strengthen his power and declared himself president for life. Papa Doc didn't believe in the army because they had held coups for all the previous presidents. He created a paramilitary group as his own private security instead of relying on the army. His security crew grew to have more power than the army and protected him from a coup by the military."

He was not an elite mulatto nor was he a poor man; he was from the slim Haitian minority—the middle class. Duvalier appealed to the black middle class by introducing public works into middle class neighborhoods that previously had been unable to have any of the necessities, including paved roads, running water, or modern sewage systems. Duvalier's policies were designed to end the dominance of the elite.

The elite were college educated, experienced business owners. While they represented about two percent of the population, they controlled over 90 percent of the money in the country. Willem explained, "The elite are the problem in Haiti. They have done little to help the country but have done everything to benefit themselves. Papa Doc went after them—kill them or make them leave the country. He wouldn't tolerate the elite. You see, it's hard to change a place like Haiti because the problems are so deep." Willem explained, "If you didn't do what Papa Doc said, he put you in jail or killed you." During his reign, he imprisoned and killed thousands of his own people in the process of making change. The poor and middle class Haitian citizens had an opportunity to conduct business and prosper under this regime, and the black middle class felt a great improvement in this time.

In 1971, shortly before his death, Papa Doc designated his son Jean Claude as his heir to head of the country. Jean Claude Duvalier, known as Baby Doc, was only nineteen-years-old when he became president. Unlike his father who had been from the middle class and was a champion of the people, Baby Doc was raised in an isolated environment, and he had never expressed interest in Haitian Politics. His father had amassed a fortune of about fourteen million dollars while the economic and political condition of the country continued to decline. Baby Doc's reign was known for intense corruption and exploitation of the poor.

In 1971 the United States feared that the African Swine Fever (ASF) disease that plagued pigs on the island would spread and devastate the U.S. hog industry. They planned to replace all native Haitian pigs with others sent by U.S. and international agencies. Baby Doc accepted this proposal and arrangements were made with American farmers, and hogs were shipped to Port-au-Prince.

Throughout the mountainous country, the black Haitian hogs were slaughtered. Then the white American-bred pigs were introduced to their new homes to replace the Haitian pigs. For the poor farmers, the pigs were their family's savings accounts and were essential to their financial security. In the eyes of the U.S. farmers and philanthropists, they had not only helped the Haitian farmers, but also protected U.S. farms. However, the tropical environment was terribly harsh on the pigs, and many of them could not tolerate the new food and indigenous parasites. They quickly became ill and many of the newly introduced pigs died. Those that survived required significantly more care than the previous animals, and the result for the poor, struggling farmers was devastating. Many families lost the equivalent of their entire savings accounts, and the rest were stuck with needy animals they had to work hard to keep alive. In the eyes of his countrymen, by giving in to U.S. pressures for this farming project, Baby Doc had effectively destroyed the economy of many Haitian farmers.

On February 7, 1986, the U.S. army forced Baby Doc into exile. Willem explained, "Baby Doc harvested what his father sowed. His father left him his fortune and a system to produce great personal wealth. When the United States forced him into exile in France, Baby Doc had obtained $800 million himself."

During the 1970s and 1980s, after Baby Doc was out of the picture, drug trafficking from Colombia to the United States became a huge problem for both countries. Willem said, "After the president was gone, the Haitian army sensed that leadership void, and they tried to get rich." As the United States stepped up efforts to eliminate the Colombian cartels, Haiti became a convenient halfway point for cocaine traffic. The drug lords obtained a foothold with the army, and Haiti quickly became a center for cocaine, which was eventually sold on the streets in the United States. Before long, the drug cartels were firmly entrenched in the street gangs of Port-au-Prince and other major Haitian cities.

Willem said, "At that point, the outside world promised lots of money. The United States and lots of other countries vowed to help. Certainly, Haiti could not get by without help. But there were some major problems with corruption in the government, and then the United States stopped giving aid because of the corruption. So what do you do? The drug dealers come in and offer money and say 'close your eyes,' and you take their money. Not only is the government corrupt, but now it is in financial relationship with drug dealers, so the outside world starts building a case against you. It's a no-win situation."

Lavalas

As we stood next to the series of photographs of the presidents, Willem discussed the aftermath of the departure of Baby Doc. The country went through a series of politically unstable regimes, moving from one military government to another. From 1986 to 1991 the country experienced numerous military coups. He turned to the image of the former Catholic priest Jean Bertrand Aristide. Willem said, "I got to know him pretty well when I was working for CNN, and I interpreted all of his interviews. When he tried to speak English, it slowed him down. But when he spoke in French or Creole, and I translated for him, I knew where he was going, and he could talk faster. He liked that. We would sit down and chat over coffee, and he was a very engaging and fun guy. We got along well, and I liked him at the beginning.

"He was a great politician. He would talk to everybody—the elite, the poor, and anybody at all. That was very different from other politicians. The upper class people would never sit and talk to these people; they would treat them like slaves. Aristide was different. He would sit down and put his arm around them. He made them feel important and like there was someone there for them. Then he could make them do whatever he wanted. He was very smart.

"When he talked to the regular people on the street he didn't talk in French, he talked like he was from the ghetto and talked in curse words. He was very, very smart. Not only did he speak seven languages, but he convinced people that he cared about them, and then they would do anything for him. He made people feel like he was their best buddy. If you brought him back now, he could be the president tomorrow."

Willem explained that Aristide promised to wash out the corruption and drug traffickers from the country just as a mudslide washes out the side of a mountain, bringing everything down with it. When storms come, and the heavy rains cause mudslides that wash out everything off a hillside; the Haitian Creole word for this phenomenon is *Lavalas*. This was his plan to bring peace and prosperity to the country, and the reason he named his new political party Lavalas. He ran for president in 1990 and won with 67 percent of the vote that international observers deemed free and fair. Since 1990, the Lavalas party has won every presidential election, but their policies have strayed far from their original intent.

After his election, Aristide got right to work to end corruption, and this made for radical policies that alarmed the country's elite. As stated by one Haitian businessman, "They wanted to help the poor. But in doing so, they were determined to make all of us poor." In his reforms and crackdowns on corruption, the restrictions on the wealthy and their businesses made it impossible for them to turn a profit. It only took ten months for the elite of Haiti to overthrow him in another violent coup; they took Aristide out of the country and imprisoned him in nearby Jamaica. Violent resistance continued, and thousands of Haitians were killed during a period of military rule. The coup created a large-scale exodus of refugees to the United States.

In September 1994, the United States stepped in to the Haitian political mess and rather than letting the country of Haiti conduct it's own business, President Bill Clinton sent the entire 82nd Airborne on the way with heavy artillery. When the leaders saw the show of force, they agreed to step down. In October, the U.S. military reinstated Aristide as president of the country.

Aristide returned to the presidency a changed man. He knew that if he continued with the sweeping reform he started, he would be assassinated. For his protection, he disbanded the Haitian army and established a civilian police force. He reversed many of his policies, made deals with the drug lords, and worked to keep the power with the elite just as Baby Doc had done. In doing so, he amassed a great personal fortune, and the country suffered terribly.

We concluded our tour of the museum and thanked our guide for his time. As we walked out, I felt enlightened by seeing firsthand so many historical artifacts; yet I was overwhelmed by the enormity of the country's problems. We went to a nearby restaurant for lunch with Willem's friend Rachael, and we continued our discussion. Rachael was happy to join in and told plenty of stories from her previous experience with the Aristide regime. "Aristide did lots of things for himself." She said, "He took $600,000 from the government and used it to buy land and build a personal mansion. When he finished the house, he turned around and sold the house to the back to government for $1,200,000. Then he kept that money and lived in the home."

I asked, "How do you know about this?"

"Oh, everybody knew about it. It was widely reported. Everybody knew about the corruption, but you couldn't do anything about it," Rachael said.

"Why not?"

"He could kill you! Oh, Aristide was very mean. You were not supposed to be against him." She went on to elaborate on Aristide's corruption. "One day there was a guy who imported trucks to sell to the government. His profits were $300,000, and Aristide asked him for the profits, but he said 'No.' A few days later, the man was kidnapped and held for ransom for the money that he owed to Aristide." Speaking as one who had been kidnapped and held for ransom herself, she had plenty of personal experience with this.

"Who did the kidnapping?" I asked.

Rachael answered, "Most of the kidnapping was orchestrated by Aristide. The police did the kidnapping, and Aristide was the chief of the kidnappers. They got the money."

Aristide also changed the national religion in Haiti from Catholicism to voodoo. Willem said, "It's not very surprising that he was in voodoo since Haitian Catholicism is so close to voodoo. And when it happened, the people didn't make a big deal about it."

Willem and Rachael ordered off the menu in French and handed the menus to the waiter, and then Willem told me that he had ordered a meal of roast goat, as well as some coffee, which he knew that I liked. Together, they explained that when Aristide's term ended in February 1996, René Préval, a prominent Aristide political ally of the Lavalas party, was elected president with 88 percent of the vote. This was Haiti's first transition between two democratically elected presidents in almost 200 years of democracy. However, Préval not only continued with Aristide's corrupt policies, but he also dismissed legislators whose terms had expired—the entire Chamber of Deputies and all but nine members of the Senate. Préval then ruled by decree rather than through democratic process. He essentially became a dictator.

In 2000, Aristide once again ran for president. This time, however, the people decided to boycott the polling booths as a means to voice their opposition. This seemed like good policy to the uneducated masses but didn't work well when the votes were counted. When the November 2000 elections were held, Aristide was again elected president, with more than 90 percent of the vote on a very low voter turnout.

In 2004, President Aristide had planned to celebrate the Haitian bicentennial at the very site where Boukman had originally inspired the Haitian revolution in a voodoo ceremony. This former Catholic priest was planning to conduct a voodoo ceremony himself in which he and his colleagues would kill a pig and drink the blood. However, the country was in the midst of such a violent uprising at the time that the roads were blocked off, and his presidential motorcade was unable to get to ceremony. Willem chuckled, "This is one time when the violence actually did something good for the country."

As we ate our goat, they continued to explain that during this period of violence, rebels burned tires in the streets and marched toward Port-au-Prince with the intention of killing the president. The United States responded this time by sending in a special forces team to the presidential palace and escorted Aristide to South Africa. Aristide claimed that he was illegally kidnapped, while the U.S. administration contends that he was being protected and that they had saved his life. Then the United Nations sent peacekeeping forces to occupy Haiti. They were there to continue the policies of Aristide, with no orders to act on the drug lords or deal with governmental corruption. They were only given legal authority to disperse violence in the streets, and they have been a presence driving around Port-au-Prince ever since then.

The next elections were held in 2006, and once again many ballots were cast blank in protest. Since the law required that the president be elected by a majority of the vote, and there were over ninety candidates running for office, the election was difficult to conduct. The decision was made to not include blank votes in the count, and with their new creative method of vote counting, the Lavalas Party representative, Préval, won with 51.5 percent of the votes. Préval took office in May 2006 and is the current president of Haiti. The armed gangs in the poor neighborhoods still wield considerable power, and the Haitian government and the UN peacekeepers have done little to change that.

I had finished my meal and cradled my cup of tepid coffee in my hands. I asked Willem, "Way out in Thomassin and Gramothe, how did the country's politics affect them?"

Sitting up straight in his chair he answered, "It affects the whole country. We might be up in the hills away from things, but the politics affect us all. You need to provide places for educated kids to get jobs. Gramothe is being educated, but tomorrow these kids need to find a job in Port-au-Prince. And since the city has been in chaos, right now they have nowhere to go."

Willem collected our empty plates, handed them to the waiter, and asked for the check. He talked about the founding of MTM in 1999, in the midst of all of this political and social disarray and how they have worked in relative peacefulness to help the village of Gramothe. Mission teams come to the country during all seasons and even during elections. Willem has managed to stay out of the political unrest while he protected his American guests from trouble by avoiding the regions of Port-au-Prince where protests and demonstrations generally take place.

Willem continued to build the community of Gramothe and find a way to succeed when everything around him seemed to be failing. He explained, "Poverty isn't about not having money. It's a mindset that takes over and changes you when your basic needs—food, water, and shelter—are not met. If you go for a long time without these things, your whole understanding of life is different. People will do whatever they can to get food. We are here to help these people meet those basic needs themselves, so that they can stand up on their own. When they see their life in Jesus as a life with a meaning beyond themselves and about giving glory to God, everything changes. When we do that while providing them with clean water and a job or an education, it's a real blessing."

Willem held his black leather wallet in his hand as he left a small stack of Haitian currency on the table. "What Haiti needs is not more government support or handouts. Those things just make us dependant. What Haiti needs is freedom and security. Along with that, education will bring jobs, which will bring overall prosperity. If MTM can display the village of Gramothe as a model for other villages to follow, then all over Haiti villages can do what we are doing, and we can defeat generational poverty village by village." Then he slapped his hands down flat on the table indicating that both the lunch and the discussion were over.

CHAPTER 4
HOPE

One man gives freely, yet gains even more;
another withholds unduly, but comes to poverty.

Proverbs 11:24

Willem continued to live among the missionaries and worked hard arranging real estate and interpreting. By the time he finished his schooling, he had bought and sold about a dozen cars and was enjoying a Toyota Four-runner as he worked for Bob Cave at the Pentecostal Holiness Mission. Willem remembered, "He hired me to work, and my job was to take care of over forty schools. I was to go all over the country to visit the schools and feeding programs once a month. It was a lot of driving."

One day, as he was driving north on National Route One, he saw a crew of white people working just beyond the road on a little compound. Ever inquisitive, he slowed down and pulled on to their property to see what they were doing. He got out of his car and surveyed the area. He saw a few buildings and between fifty and sixty American missionaries. Willem walked along a dusty path and struck up a conversation with some men who were taking a break under a banana tree. They told him that they were working with Hope Mission Tours (the name was later changed to Hope Mission Outreach). Bob and Sharon Johnson, who were from Indiana, led this organization. They had been in Haiti since 1972 and had a vision for a church, school, and medical clinic.

Within a few minutes, he tracked down Sharon who invited him to have a seat and a cup of coffee.

Willem said, "I really appreciate the work you are doing here to help the Haitian people."

She looked him in the eye and said, "Son, I've been out here working for years, and this is the first time someone stopped and encouraged me in what I'm doing here." She paused and looked over this clean cut, well-dressed young man and said, "Who are you?"

Willem introduced himself. "I'm Willem Charles. I work for the Pentecostal Holiness Mission, and I'm in charge of their schools."

She replied, "Son, God told me something I'm about to share with you."

Willem raised his eyebrows, "What?"

She said, "You are going be working for me." Willem replied, "Oh, no. I don't think so."

She said, "Son, you know what? I saw you when you pulled your car in, and I knew there was something about you. Then when you got out of the car, and God told me that you were going to be working for me."

Willem grinned. After a little more casual discussion, they exchanged contact information, and he headed home. About five months later, Willem's time with the Pentecostal Holiness Mission came to an end, and he wrote Sharon a letter saying that he was free to help them, if they were still interested.

Upon receiving the letter, she picked up the phone and called him. She said, "Willem, hi. I just got your letter. I told you so."

They met, and she gave Willem a quick tour of the compound and introduced him to her husband, Bob. He said, "The first time I met Willem, he struck me as a gentleman. Willem was intelligent and had an ability to get things done. He acted more like an American than a Haitian. He also thought more like an American and was able to put things together and accomplish things. Most Haitians were looking for a meal, but he wasn't one of those. He was looking to see what he could build."

Sharon said, "What impressed me was his personality, cleanliness, and his English. Hope Missions held crusade services and conducted a lot of personal evangelism where he interpreted for us. He interpreted for us in all situations. Not only did he interpret, but if we wanted money changed at the appropriate exchange rate, he would take care of it. If we wanted to go to a village for a crusade, he would talk to the village leaders, arrange it, and then do the interpreting."

Willem worked with Sharon closely for a number of years and listened to her, as a son listens to the counsel of his mother. Hope had Americans and Canadians coming down for short-term mission trips all the time. "When people want to come, we take whoever has the heart to go," Sharon said. "We don't screen them and ask what denomination they are or anything because we know Jesus has chosen them and our calling is to be transporters of people. Just be like the Nike check mark and do something. People sit around and talk and talk, but all I'm saying is do something to make a difference. I'm not a fan of church committees. It's like we have to talk about it for six months before we can do anything. I tell you, I've been set free from that. I serve an all-inclusive Jesus, and he set me free. I'm not gonna be bound down by labels or chains. I'll always live outside the box. I'm a very impatient person. If there's a need I want to meet it right away, I don't want to wait until the committee says it's okay."

Sharon remembered, "We've had a lot of good talks." Once, Willem was working with an American girl who had a shapely, plump physique. Willem thought that her family was rich because in Haiti plumpness suggested that a person had enough money to eat very well. Haitian men also seem to find large women attractive. At one point, Willem was talking with her about why she was still single. He said very pleasantly, "You'll easily find a man to marry. Look at how fat you are!" He gave an innocent smile, but she turned and walked away. Sharon overheard the conversation and came to the rescue of the young girl. After a discussion of some pertinent cultural differences, they had a pleasant laugh and no harm was done.

Willem discussed with Sharon his previous relationship he had with the missionary girl, and she knew that at some point, they would have to talk seriously about it. She waited, however, watching him closely as he interacted with teams of men and women, and boys and girls for months before she addressed the issue. After several months, she discussed the issue of girls with him.

Sharon remembered, "When he was younger, he sowed some wild oats like a lot of us did. So I asked him, 'What makes you not tempted now with girls?' His response was, 'Sharon, I couldn't do that to the Holy Spirit. I could not ever hurt the Holy Spirit like I did.'

Many years later, Sharon looked back and said, "You know, he calls me Mom, and he's my son. Our hearts are connected through the Holy Spirit. I trust him to this day. If I was in trouble, and I needed anything in Haiti, I would call Willem Charles, and he would take care of it for me."

Medical Clinic

When Willem started there, Hope had twenty acres and a couple of basic multipurpose buildings that they used for church and medical supplies. They did not have a formal clinic but worked out of makeshift clinics everywhere they went by bringing in nurses and doctors with lots of medicines in their luggage. One of the first things Willem helped build was a permanent medical clinic, where they could treat patients and keep their medical supplies.

When the American doctors were scheduled to hold the clinic, Willem made announcements in the village and surrounding areas, and people showed up in droves. The crowds were incredible, and they quickly dealt with all kinds of problems. Just like anywhere that resources are scarce, and people are desperate; crowds tend to get unruly and even violent. Willem developed a system for crowd control. Every patient got a ticket and specific rules were applied to the waiting area, such as No getting out of line and No fighting. Enforcement of the rules sometimes involved shutting down the clinic for the day.

The clinic became very influential, not only for the individuals who received medical care that they otherwise would not have been able to afford, but as a means to spread the word of Hope Missions. By offering this much-needed service, Hope Missions became well known, leading to more opportunities for crusades to share the gospel of Jesus Christ in other villages near and far.

At the clinics, they would have around 500 people show up each morning. At the end of the day, those at the end of the line went home without seeing a doctor. On the last day of the clinic, hundreds didn't receive care. The day after the medical team left, another several hundred people continued to show up each day in hopes that they could be treated. Willem had the undesirable job of explaining that the American doctors had left and another team would be coming in a few weeks.

Later, he sat quietly pondering about the hundreds he had turned away, and he wondered how much of a difference they were actually making. Sharon sat with him and told him a story. "You know there was a little boy walking along the edge of the ocean after the tide had gone out, and hundreds of starfish were washed up on the shore. He felt bad for the starfish, and picked one up and threw it back into the ocean. He smiled and picked up another one. He continued throwing the starfish back one-by-one for hours. An old man was sitting nearby watching the little boy, and he came over to him and said, 'Son, look around. There are thousands of starfish here. Do you think you can really make a difference by throwing a couple back?' The boy looked at the man, picked up another starfish, held it in his hand, and looked at it closely before throwing it back into the tumbling waves. Then he said, 'I made a difference for that one.'" Sharon paused and looked at Willem. "There will always be more to do, but we have to treat people one at a time and make a difference for each one. You invest, you invest, and you trust. And God honors that." Sharon got up and walked away leaving Willem encouraged and ready to go another day.

Here Comes the Army

Sharon reminisced about Willem's work at Hope, "He managed the complex that we were building, and he seemed to know just about everybody you would need to know in the government to get things done. We just shared with him our dreams and our visions, which included the dream for a school. I was so impressed with him right from the start." Bob and Sharon also went back and forth between Haiti and their home in the States on a regular basis, leaving Willem to run the mission in their absence.

The United States Army had established a presence in Haiti during the political instability in the early 1990s. They had plenty of men, trucks, and supplies, but after the initial stabilization, the men in the army didn't have much to do. Willem knew a number of Americans in the army and spent some time with them. They told him that the army was planning to do some humanitarian aid after things calmed down. They said, "We're out here and not very busy, could we build something?"

Willem talked with them about Hope Missions and proposed that they build a school. The army agreed to supply the building materials and enlisted their men to do the labor. With his plan in mind, Willem called Bob and Sharon who were in the States at the time. He explained that he had made all the arrangements, and if they agreed to it, they could have a school built at no charge. They pondered this new growth opportunity but were a little hesitant because although a school was certainly part of their plan, they had no means of supporting the school once it was built. They didn't have teachers lined up, school supplies, or any administrative necessities. Sharon, in her characteristic spontaneity encouraged her husband, "Bob, if God can give us the school, then he will certainly supply the money and people to keep it running. Let him do it, Bob."

The army got busy right away. They donated a couple of trucks and put their men to work. They pitched an army tent on the property until the school was built. They spent over $300,000 in the compound and in the process built a school, basketball court, and dug a well. It was all American material, and the mission wasn't charged a dime. Not long after it was built, they managed to open the school, and it has been providing Haitian kids with a quality Christian education ever since.

In addition to the school, most of the activity at Hope Missions centered around short-term mission teams coming, especially with medical and evangelistic teams. Ministry ramped up when teams were present and faded out when they were absent. Willem saw the need to be consistent in ministry with local pastors whether a team was there or not. He helped start a Bible study and brought in pastors from all over the surrounding regions every Saturday. They challenged one another and dug into the Bible as a group. Under Willem leadership this engaging and encouraging group stayed together for many years.

Beth

The fourth child in string of five, Beth Tyron came from a modest family in Terre Haute, Indiana. "My father's idea of vacation with all us the kids and a slim budget was to go camping. We did it in a very primitive way, which was Dad's thing to do. I washed dishes in cold water using a bucket and was pretty well acclimated to primitive living ever since I could remember. My father is a hard-working man who believes that is how you get ahead in life, and my mother has always been the queen of improvising. They were my foundation. When you add all the things you go through as a single mother who has struggled through a marriage, it's amazing how God builds our character and prepares us for what he wants us to do. I am who I am."

In 1990 Beth was working full time and going to school full time at a local technical college for a two-year associates degree in computer-aided graphic design. Beth said, "I had come back to the Lord and decided that I had wasted enough of God's time and wanted to get busy." She began by supporting the missionary that her church supported, and she signed up for training at Terre Haute Church of God, where she quickly became a member. She completed the new beginners programs at the church, was water baptized, and went through two more discipleship courses. She completed the intense ministerial internship program the Church of God uses for comprehensive discipleship training and ordaining their ministers. Having been divorced she was not eligible for ordination, but she did complete up to the exhorters license, which was only one step below becoming ordained.

Beth explained, "I had a heart for children. It was through child evangelism fellowship I came to know the Lord at the age of nine. When I came back to the Lord, I felt that he had placed in my heart a desire to minister to children. So I went to my pastor and said, 'I need to be plugged into ministry, and I want to minister to kids, but my calling is not within the four walls of the church.'"

Beth developed a plan that she called the Big Ten Club. It mirrored the image of Big Ten basketball, which runs deep in Indiana. They met the kids playing sports for ten weeks and covered the Ten Commandments, as well as the gospel of Jesus Christ. But Beth didn't want to limit the program to kids in the church; she wanted to meet the poor kids downtown. Beth met with the Terre Haute housing authority and shared her vision. They loved her plan and gave her the use of one of their facilities. Within a couple of weeks, she was off and running.

"We were ministering to lots of kids, and the majority were black. Kids that were involved in sports, and once they were there, they had lots of fun and learned the gospel also. The program was a big success. In time, it spread to another housing projects in Terre Haute." The program was aimed at reaching the whole city and was not limited to one church, so Beth presented her vision to other churches in town; she worked closely with a number of people at Mt. Pleasant Church and Calvary Temple of Terre Haute. These churches allowed the ministry to use their van and a number of people volunteered to help. Soon the program overgrew its facilities, and they started taking the kids to churches.

Beth recalled, "I had a really good friend who was black, and she introduced me to an area of Terre Haute that was known as a place where white people were not supposed to be. She took me there, and I won favor, was walking the streets, and everybody thought I was nuts. We would go out on the streets on Friday night with our fliers and let kids know about what we were doing. It was a lot of fun. I had the hand of God upon me, and I had my girlfriend and the people she trusted were there, so I felt totally secure." As a white girl from the Midwest this project exposed Beth to things she had never dealt with before, and she loved it. She said, "When I came to Haiti, nothing was new to me."

In 1993, feeling a desire to help beyond the borders of Terre Haute, Beth was excited when she heard of a mission trip to Haiti led by a young pastor from Danville Chapel named Roger Stoup. Roger had met Bob and Sharon Johnson when they had spoken at his church the year before. He organized a team to visit, and Beth wanted to be a part of it. On her second day at Hope Missions, Beth met the energetic young man who was interpreting for the team. Willem didn't simply interpret but helped in any way that was needed for the ministry. Roger commented, "My first impression was that he was sharp," Roger said. "I was impressed by his understanding of colloquialisms. He was definitely the best of their interpreters."

Willem and Beth hit it off immediately. She saw in Willem a man who wanted to do ministry as much as she did. Roger noted that they were inseparable during her two-week visit, and he was pleased to see how well Beth and Willem got along. On the plane ride back to the states, Roger commented to his wife that Willem and Beth would be married within a year. As it turned out, it took two years for this long-distance relationship to transform into an international marriage. Under Sharon's watchful eye, Willem inquired if she had any advice on the progress of the relationship. She advised Willem to take it slow, and if it were to develop, then it would be worth the wait. She helped them work through how Willem's previous relationship would affect them and encouraged Willem to visit her family. As Sharon said, "There were people who were against it, since it was an interracial marriage, but that was their thing to work out."

Willem recalled, "Sharon is like my mom. That's the best way to tell you who she is to me. When I was getting married, she did not let me pick. She told me, 'This is the woman you are going to get married to.' And I listened. That's how much respect I had for her."

Sharon took steps for that to happen. In order for the relationship to advance, Willem needed to visit the States and spend a little time with Beth's family, but this required a visa for Willem to travel. Willem needed a sponsor to obtain the visa, someone who would take responsibility for him and guarantee his return to Haiti, but this was a problem. A young man who speaks English is a huge risk to take in obtaining a visa. The odds are that he would not return to Haiti, and find a job and have a very comfortable life in the States instead. And the person who sponsored his visa would have to answer to the Haitian government. This is not an unfounded worry among missionaries; stories of this happening are common with missionaries who try to help young Haitians. In fact, over the years, Willem had encountered numerous people who promised that they would help him get his green card or visa, but these promises were unfulfilled over and over again.

Bob and Sharon knew the risks, but they trusted this young Haitian man and went out on a limb by sponsoring his visa. She explained, "We felt that Willem was worth the investment, and it was worth it to get him to the States." Despite some hurdles to overcome, Willem and Beth were engaged and planned a wedding on a beach resort in Haiti.

On May 26, 1994, the day before Mother's Day in Haiti, Willem and Beth had an appointment with a judge to conduct the official legal ceremony, which was separate from the wedding celebration. They traveled to Petionville and visited the small legal office where the judge filled out all of the paperwork and got everything ready for the signatures. Essentially, all that had to be done next was for the bride and groom to sign the papers, but the judge paused and said, "Okay, just a minute." He got up from his desk, turned around, and rummaged through his closet. On a shelf was a small collection of hats. He picked up a brown felt hat and looked at it carefully then shook his head and set it back down. He went on to the next and again, frowned, and set it back on the plywood shelf. He finally pulled out a tweed trilby and, pleased that this was the right one for the occasion, put it on his head. Then he sat down and announced, "Now we can commence." He went on with the process and handed the pen to Willem for the processing of the legal marriage paperwork. On June 30, 1994, they held a beautiful religious ceremony at Wahoo Bay Beach on north shores of Haiti.

After they were married, Beth moved to Haiti permanently and lived in Thomassin with Willem while they worked together full time at Hope Missions. Willem continued the legal immigration process working with the U.S. embassy and Haitian government over the following years. Knowing practically everybody in the embassy, he sailed through the process required for obtaining U.S. citizenship on his own and became a dual citizen of the United States and Haiti.

Baby Hope

On July 20, 1995, a group of about sixty people were working diligently at Hope Mission Outreach. The medical clinic was very busy, and Sharon was there when a heavily pregnant lady named Julian came in. She was obviously in labor and needed immediate attention. They brought together all the supplies they could and managed to deliver the baby right there. During the birthing process, they found out that the mother was HIV positive. This made quite a stir because a number of people had been exposed to HIV positive blood. They managed to arrange for testing for all the team members, and they also had an HIV positive baby to deal with. The mother had two other children to care for and was adamant that this baby be adopted.

Sharon said, "We named her Hope after Hope Missions and went to work to get her adopted. Willem took us down to the embassy and showed us how to do it. It seemed like he knew just about everybody you would need to know. You have to go to the consular first, so we did that with Willem's help. We just went in and said, 'We have a baby and need a medical visa.' Willem is as crazy as I am! He believes that you can do anything, just go do it!"

Two weeks later another group came through, and Bob managed to return home to the States with that group to care for baby Hope. Bob kept the precious little baby in their home in the States for five months. He took her to a doctor, and she had an examination and blood tests; she was tested HIV positive. To the Johnson family, that didn't make a difference. They kissed her, fed her, and loved her just as if she were their own. They all loved her and wanted to raise her, but they knew she needed a younger couple to bring her into their own family.

They reached out to people for adoption and had a number of people come to talk with them. Sharon told the story, "We had teachers and other good people who wanted to adopt her, but when they came and held the little baby many said they couldn't do it. They were saying, 'People will talk' or 'She's black and HIV positive' and even, 'If I do this, I might lose my job'. But finally we had a couple that wanted to adopt her, and I told them, 'She's a black girl from Haiti, and she's HIV positive.' That didn't bother them at all. They were in the medical profession. I also explained, 'This little one was anointed with oil from the time she was two weeks old. When she was brought into the States, and I do know, the Lord has given me this, that whoever adopts her, when the adoption takes place, she would be healed.' They wanted her before Christmas 1995, and we managed to get the adoption done. I got a call from her mom in February, and she said, 'She's negative. The HIV is gone. Hope and I are just dancing around here, and we're fine.' It was a miracle. You know with medical things the intellect tries to get in the way, and we try to figure things out. Let's just go back to the basics. Jesus' word is simple, and he says we need to have childlike faith."

Once she was adopted, the family had to go through a lot of paperwork to complete the adoption process. They kept her name Hope and took her mother's name Julian as the middle name. Since this was not a closed adoption, Bob and Sharon have continued to be a part of Hope's life, and even spent Thanksgiving 2009 with her. She is a straight-A student in a good Christian family and is not on any medication at all—completely free of HIV. Hope's parents are missionaries who regularly travel to the city of Cap Haitian along with Hope. And have even lived there for a few years.

A couple of years after baby Hope was born, her biological mother, Julian, died from AIDS. Her oldest son, Tony, was fourteen at the time, and he came to the mission and said, "My mother died, and I have two younger brothers, and I don't know what to do." Brad took Tony and these little boys in and they became the first kids in their new orphanage. Tony and his brothers were adopted by loving families in the states. Tony, who is now studying to be a doctor in Texas, has continued to keep in contact with his sister Hope over Facebook.

Bob and Sharon's son, Brad, has worked hard to develop the orphanage over the years and has taken in many other children. These kids, who otherwise would be left on the street or sold into a slavery type of environment, have a home that is safe where they are well-fed and go to school. The Hope orphanage is not primarily for the purpose of adopting the kids away from Haiti and taking children to the States, but rather to educate and train them in Haiti so that they can stay in their home country and be a positive influence in Haiti.

Sharon commented on the whole process, "Even now with our clinic, we need to have paperwork. People think that since it's a third world country you can go in and say, 'I want that baby' and they can take it. Well, it's not that easy. We are an NGO (nongovernmental organization), and we have the appropriate paperwork which we follow. I personally don't like all the paperwork and rules, that's one of the advantages of getting older is that you can get away with things and people just say, 'Well don't mind her because she's just getting older.' I tend to just say 'Let's do it', and we'll work out the details later. Sometimes I have to pay the consequences for that, but if you don't do anything, it will never get done. If I hadn't had Willem in my corner in 1995, we would never have been able get the paperwork done. With baby Hope, it worked."

A Graceful Exit

In 1998, Willem had been with Mission of Hope for almost a decade and had been the right-hand man to Bob and Sharon for the majority of that time. Their son, Brad had been working closely with the mission, and when he graduated from college, he moved to Hope Mission Outreach full time. He was positioned to take over and had the blessing of his parents, who were looking to continue with their ministry in the States. Willem and Brad were both strong personalities and didn't see eye to eye on everything. They talked about what direction to take, and eventually Willem choose to take an exit and head out on his own. There were no hard feelings in the process, and Willem and Beth stay in close contact with Brad, Sharon, and Bob to this day.

Sharon said, "Willem is not with us now, but I praise God because if we had not parted ways in ministry, Willem never would have made MTM without venturing out in faith and starting a ministry up there in the mountains. It's not about me. It's how we can win Haiti for Christ more effectively. Willem is a very special boy, and I knew that from the very moment he stopped in and began talking with us. Just knew it in my heart, and I took him in my heart from the very first day."

Willem shared in her sentiments. "Bob and Sharon are people that played a big role in my life. The work that we do here at MTM—I have to tell you, they get a lot of credit because I learned a lot from them."

Hope Mission Outreach continues to be a blessing to the people of Haiti. Brad and his wife, Vanessa, have worked hard for the Haitian people. They have also started Haiti One Alliance, a ministry designed to coordinate the efforts of mission organizations throughout Haiti. Willem believes strongly in their mission and has joined their efforts. MTM is a charter member of Haiti One Alliance.

CHAPTER 5
NEW BEGINNINGS

All hard work brings a profit, but mere talk leads only to poverty.

Proverbs 14:23

CNN

Hope Missions Outreach held a crusade with American pastors who came and gave a beautiful evangelistic message while Willem translated. After one of the services, a Haitian woman came up to Willem and said, "Your English is good. With all the news currently going on, CNN is looking for good translators. Why don't you see if you can work for them? You may even make good money."

Willem drove to the Hotel Montana in Port-au-Prince. He was impressed with the beautiful building, which was known as the nicest hotel in the country. Hillary Clinton had stayed there, as had many other dignitaries. In this hotel, CNN, ABC, and CBS had set up their headquarters. He asked at the front desk for the CNN office and was directed to a room down the hall; he knocked on the door. When a woman opened the door, he said in clear English, "I understand that you are looking for translators." Willem looked around the suite and recognized several of the translators who were there. He knew these young men and women from his experience of hiring and firing translators for

Hope Missions Outreach and other organizations over the previous years.

They had a discussion in which she quickly assessed the extent of his English skills. After a few minutes she said, "You're hired."

Willem said, "Okay, but I can't work for you on Saturday because every Saturday I have a Bible study. I have been leading that Bible study for years, and I don't want to give that up." His work with Bob and Sharon Johnson included a discipleship group with local pastors every Saturday, and Willem was confident that he could continue to lead that group and interpret for CNN as well.

She said, "Well, if you work for the media, you work twenty-four hours a day, and that's just the way it is. You have to work all the time."

Willem said, "By the way, I have to go to church on Sunday, too, so I can't work on Sunday."

She said, "I'm sorry. You can't be hired."

He replied, "Well, you'll lose a good translator."

She said, "What makes you think you are so good?"

He answered, "The guys you have working for you," he paused and pointed his right index finger at various people around the room naming them one by one as they stared directly at him. "They used to work for me. But I'm better than them."

She looked inquisitively at this bold young man and said, "Let's go." Instantly she headed down the hallway, and Willem followed. They met up with a small video crew and went to the parking lot where they climbed into a CNN van. She drove Willem to the military headquarters where she had an appointment for an interview. The two-story rectangular white building sat just across the street from the presidential palace and was within a stone's throw of the statue honoring an unknown Haitian freedom fighter (Negre Marron) blowing a conch shell towards the sky in a rallying call for freedom. This statue signified the beginning of the Haitian rebellion, which resulted in Haiti's independence. They parked across the street from the statue and entered the military headquarters.

The meeting was scheduled with a general in the army. They went past security, up the stairs and down the hall to the general's private office. The general's secretary checked her schedule and waved them inside, where they waited for the general. Willem grinned widely as they entered the general's office, he strolled slowly behind the mahogany desk and sat in the general's leather chair and leaned back with his hands interlaced behind his head. The CNN reporter and camera crew thought he was absolutely insane! The crew shifted around nervously, not wanting to upset the entire Haitian military. The boss stepped toward him and was about to reprimand him when the door flew open and a tall black man in a starched uniform entered the room in a brisk march. He looked at the youngster behind his desk and blurted out, "Willem, my boy. It's so good to see you!"

The general had been a neighbor of Willem's in Thomassin. They played soccer together and over the last several years had become friends. In fact Willem had been to that very office before to visit. Willem chatted with the general before the meeting. The official interview lasted about ten minutes; it was Willem's first official duty for CNN. The crew seemed shocked and was probably wondering just who Willem was.

There wasn't much discussion on the way back to the hotel. The news that they had captured in the interview was plain vanilla and would result in a routine report. The real news to the chief was this crazy Haitian interpreter who knew everybody, including the general, and spoke perfect English. When they got back she said, "You're hired. I will give you a car so you can go to your Saturday Bible study. What time does you Bible study start?"

Willem said, "Two o'clock."

She said, "You can leave at about one and then come back to work at four or five. And on Sunday, you go to church, and after church you get back to work."

Willem said, "That's fine with me."

A couple hours later at the Hotel Montana, the television sets were airing the story featuring the general's interview. Everybody in the suite was watching. While there was nothing shocking about the news, the people in the newsroom were watching the talented young man take on the intonation and character of the general himself. Willem had just solidified his role on staff at CNN.

Willem excused himself from the newsroom and took a stroll through the office. He looked around and saw piles of empty water bottles with no ice, and there was no potable water to be found. The office was a mess with papers and trash strewn about and interpreters standing idly waiting for assignments. He went outside and made an assessment of the fleet of about forty cars and vans outside. With his notebook in hand, he wrote down license plate numbers and made notes on the condition of the vehicles. Most of the vehicle's gas tanks were on empty, and a couple had obvious mechanical problems. He made an assessment of the thirty-five Haitian drivers and the crew of about forty-five Americans working along side them. He found the schedule, which listed current projects and assignments, and it didn't take long for him to notice large gaps in the day when little work was getting done.

Willem made notes on all of these things and went to the boss's office later in the afternoon. He said, "You have all of these people and a very impressive hotel. But when you look around at this office, you have some problems. You don't have any ice or water. Your vehicles are a mess, and many of them have no gas." He went on and listed all the problems that he saw and explained how it could be better, holding nothing back from his initial assessment. Then he handed her his paper that listed all the issues he had just mentioned. She paused and held the paper loosely in her hand and looked carefully at Willem. Who was this man who came into her operation and saw through the administrative problems so quickly? She said, "You are in charge now." And she called all of the interpreters over and announced, "From now on, Willem is in charge."

Willem became the CNN coordinator in Haiti. He made all the arrangements for the translators and assigned the translators as they routinely gathered information on the street. He personally translated major stories that were on television. In the process of working there, since much of the news was about the political instability, he met and interpreted for the current president, Jean-Bertrand Aristide, as well as the future president, Rene Préval. Aristide's right-hand man, Pere Jean-Juste, was always present before and after any interaction that the president had with the media. Willem took special care of him and personally took him back home at night in his own vehicle. At one point during Aristide's presidency, Jean-Juste told Aristide, "We're not going to leave Willem behind."

Aristide replied, "He's going to come work for me then."

Willem simply smiled and didn't say anything. Saying no to that offer would have meant saying no to Aristide, which is something that was simply not done.

Willem continued working for CNN for about a year making good money—anywhere from $300 to $500 a day; he often worked overtime for extra money. He continued to work for Bob and Sharon Johnson, maintained the pastor's Saturday Bible study, and occasionally placed missionaries in homes. When Hope Missions Outreach brought teams in for a week, his life was quite busy, and juggling his various responsibilities was tricky to say the least.

Willem's Home

Willem poured the money he was making into building a new house. He bought just over an acre in Thomassin forty-eight and thought about what he would like to have for a home. He had constructed buildings before and was familiar with the process, but this was to be his own home. He thought about it for some time and worked out the general plan in his mind then called together a handful of skilled workers to begin the building process.

The very first thing that must be done whenever a building is constructed is to dig out a cistern for water. This cistern will provide the water necessary for the construction, as well as be a long-term source of water for the home. Willem tasked his crew with digging a seventeen-by-twenty-foot cistern that was about eight feet deep. Using pick axes and shovels, they dug and leveled the land and made a concrete floor, walls, and ceiling to create the 20,000-gallon cistern. Willem kept the rocks removed in construction of the cistern and used them to line the cistern, build a ten-foot wall around the property, and construct the foundation of the house; there were plenty left to fashion the bearing wall of the house. All of the rocks they needed for building the house came from the ground on which it sat. He saved huge amounts of money using the existing rock, which minimized the cost of purchasing and hauling in rock or cement blocks. The only foreign rock he used was beautiful pink sandstone for the front wall of the home.

This was not simply Willem's home, but the home for his new bride, as well as temporary quarters for countless guests over the years. Beth, being an independent American woman, drew up her plans for the house on paper. But in a culture where they don't use paper, the result was not exactly what she had envisioned. She said, "I would give them a drawing and explain what we wanted. But a six-foot hallway somehow becomes a fourteen-foot hallway. So, you just have to be at the work site all the time."

And they were the majority of the time. Interspersed among Willem's numerous activities, he always managed to start and end the day with the construction crew. Once the foundation was complete, the cistern was chlorinated so the water could be used for daily household water; drinking water was purchased through Culligan.

The home was under construction for the next year and eventually became known as the Guest House Thomassin. This comfortable home has housed visitors from all around the world. Taking a walk through the backyard reveals Beth's green thumb. "We have three avocado trees. One was here before we were. Another produces annually, and another is a Jerusalem avocado, which grows basketball-sized fruit." She shrugged a little and continued, "We have not seen them yet on our tree because this is the first year it will produce. But we do have oranges—Haiti is home to several varieties of oranges. Three of the orange trees were supposed to be sweet oranges, but turned out to be a very acidic orange that grows here. This orange is used for cleaning pots and for cleaning meat. The meat butchered on the street isn't the cleanest, and it has flies. The lack of refrigeration means you can't just cook it and eat it. So they sanitize the meat with this orange. When the chicken that you eat here tastes a little like lemon or that flavor you can't quite put your finger on, that's what it is. When you've lived here long enough, all the meat starts tasting the same because they use the same spices and clean it with the same oranges."

Beth continued through her garden, "We have a cherry tree that has produced like three cherries one time. So I'm still waiting on it. And we have my favorite tree, which I call my never-die tree. In Haiti they call it Ben Olive, but the actual marketing name is the moringa tree. This tree is totally edible—its pods are harvested, and they are much like okra. They've also been likened to asparagus because it is long and thin. You can eat the leaves raw in salad or you can boil them for stews and sauces or cat it like spinach. It's very high in protein. The seed that I grew mine from actually was harvested from La Gonaives, a little island off the coast of Haiti, and shipped to Miami, Florida, to a nonprofit organization that distributes these seeds to third world countries.

"Willem has an aunt who raises cows up in the mountains. I gave seedlings of this tree to his aunt who planted them on the mountain. This tree does not make good firewood, therefore they tend to leave it alone when they need firewood."

Poverty throughout the country has caused people to do anything to survive. This includes cutting down trees to sell, use as firewood, or turn into charcoal. When an entire nation does this over the course of generations, deforestation results. Hillsides have become depleted of trees and the valuable roots that hold the soil. The erosion that ensues has caused entire mountainsides to wash away under hard rains. Arial photographs show desolate landscape with the appearance of strip mines.

This has spawned a subset of mission work focused on reforestation. Trees are distributed to the peasants to offset deforestation. Botanists, working alongside existing mission organizations, have helped distribute and plant trees. A friend of Willem's who was working with a Haiti reforestation project took a few branches right from Beth's tree, and he planted them; they are flourishing. The biggest challenge with projects of this sort is education. Some organizations were faced with peasants who thought the trees were a trick to make their lives more miserable. They said they wanted fruit trees, but instead, they got trees they considered useless. This was because the trees were new to them, and they didn't know their usefulness. Cultural differences and short-term relationships have frustrated projects like this.

Beth continued talking about her favorite tree, "Now, the never-die part of it is that the tree in our yard has been blown over three times when we've been away for the summer. Each time, we just break off a piece, and stick it in the ground, and it grows back up again."

Several large green banana plants occupy the corners of Beth's garden. Graceful leaves up to nine feet long and two feet wide shade the walkway beneath them. A variety of species including plantains (cooking bananas) fill the corners of the garden. A grove of palm trees line the driveway and round out the tropical feeling of the landscape.

The house has been Willem and Beth's home for a dozen years, and they had been hosting people even before it was completely finished. "Now," Willem explained. "With all the comforts available, people pay $420 for a week's stay in the Guest House Thomassin. That covers all the expense of having a team stay. It's not a bad deal. Where else can you stay for a whole week, with free wireless Internet access and two hot meals a day, for only $420?"

For many years, Willem and Beth lived out their lives right in front of the visitors who graced their home. Rarely did they have a moment to themselves. Willem used the profits derived from the Guest House to build a separate home solely for his family just downhill from the Guest House. Willem was also able to purchase another small house with the intent of renting it. Over the years, he has rented the house to missionaries, but has also served as a storage area for a variety of items for MTM.

When asked if missionaries should take a vow of poverty and be poor in order to minister to the poor, Willem simply replied, "If a missionary has no money, then how can they help anybody? I would think that we would want missionaries to be prosperous and have connections with other prosperous people."

Willem has made business opportunities out of doors that have opened for him. At the same time, he has been mindful to be generous, by giving away his interpreting services to missionaries continuously over the years. When asked about his personal finances, Willem said, "I'm the kind of guy who never wants to be in a position where people take the credit for making me well off. You know what I'm saying? When Abram rescued Lot with all the women and the other people in the battle, he gave the guy Melchizedek a tenth of everything that he got in the plunder. Then Abram said to the king of Sodom, 'I will not accept anything belonging to you, so that you will never be able to say, 'I made Abram rich." In the same way, I will not accept money from people who want to have control. When people give, they give to God, and God blesses in return. I need to be better off in a good way without cheating, or without anyone else having control."

"You can see the way MTM is. If people who are not living here and involved on a day-to-day basis controlled MTM, it would not be what it is today. It would be like so many other ministries that go by the wayside once the founder moves out. The people don't feel the ownership because it's not theirs. MTM is God's ministry and, God willing, it will last to serve the next generation as well."

New Birth

In 1998, Willem had made considerable headway on his home. He resigned from his position at CNN and shortly after that, made his exit from Hope Missions Outreach. Late one evening, he sat on stackable plastic chair on the concrete slab that would one day become his back porch. There was no breeze, and it was a perfect seventy-one degrees as he looked over the river to a small flat region on the opposite hillside. He remembered playing there with his childhood friend Larry Jr. many years ago. Willem knew the men and women of the village having grown up together and even played with many of them when they were kids. He pondered the area and the village that evening with the sun at his back as it cast its final rays before it hid for the night behind the mountain.

He was drawn to the village in a way he couldn't explain. After sitting and thinking about it for a long time, he finally retired to what turned out to be a restless night. He thought about what he had seen over the past decade at Hope Mission Outreach. The gospel of Jesus Christ had changed lives, and schools had given hope to villages where there had never been schools before. He had seen medical treatments help thousands of people. He knew the influence that a well-run, gospel-oriented mission could have on a local community. And right here behind his home, was a village that was desperate for help.

The following day, he awoke early and went for a hike. He walked down the hill, across the river and up to the village of Gramothe to speak with his friends there. The river isolated the village geographically and almost nothing substantial was to be found in Gramothe. He climbed the hill to see a collage of scattered homes built from sheet metal. Children were playing soccer along the path. The youngest were naked. Men, unable to find work, sat on their front steps. Because it was the dry season, fields sat idle. They would have to wait for six months for the rain to come, so they could plant their crops. There was one small "school" with nineteen children and a poorly educated teacher. A supply house in the middle of the village sold a variety of household items. Five voodoo temples were scattered through the village, their flags clearly visible. By all accounts it was a village without hope—a place where some 2,500 people struggled to get by.

But, everywhere he looked, Willem saw potential. Through visionary eyes, he saw a church that proclaimed the gospel of Jesus Christ and baptized believers in the name of the Father, the Son, and the Holy Spirit. He saw a school, which provided a quality education supported by loving North Americans who sponsored children, giving them hope for careers beyond the confines of the village. He saw a medical clinic and even a hospital to care for the sick and injured. He saw farms that were prospering and a paved road carrying trucks full of harvested crops from the village to the market. He saw a village with hope and a future that could be used as a model for other villages. He saw Haitians helping Haitians, and a community with jobs and opportunities that was self-supporting for the first time in hundreds of years. He saw a people with a deep love for Jesus Christ who had defeated generational poverty.

Willem looked into the eyes of the elders of the village and announced, "I'm going to start a church and a school here."

CHAPTER 6
LET'S GO TO SCHOOL

Train a child in the way he should go, and
when he is old he will not turn from it.

Proverbs 22:6

When Willem approached the men and women of Gramothe and told them his plans to build a church and a school, some laughed at him. Others sat back and watched to see if this energetic young man had the determination and capacity to accomplish such an audacious task. There were two families in the village that had been Christians for several years, and they were frustrated with the lack of a local church. They had been making the three-hour walk to the church in Fermat each week. They said to Willem, "If you build a church here, we'll stay and help you."

That spurred Willem on and fueled the fire in his heart to see it through. Initially, the need was for a school and right along with that comes the church. In Haiti, it's almost automatic that if you have a church, then you also have a school. They traditionally operate as a single entity, and the pastor runs everything. So, the villagers knew that when the church was being built, a school was going to come right along with it.

Start with What's There

In the spring of 1999, Willem and Beth began organizing the process for conducting their school, but, technically, there was a school there in the village already. It was a very small effort held in one lady's home. The teacher wasn't the best qualified, but she was all they could get right there in the village, and she was willing and wanted to help the children. So these nineteen children of Gramothe were in a school, of sorts. Willem started by helping the teacher. He met with her and found out what she needed and how she was being supported. The student's families were supposed to be paying her, but often the payments didn't come; the money she received barely covered any of the costs associated with caring for the children, and she struggled to get paper and markers for the kids. The school had no books and seemed more like a day care. She loved the kids and was teaching out of the goodness of her heart. Without her, nobody would be teaching these precious children.

Willem painted a big picture as he talked with her. He envisioned a large school with teachers for each class level, a library, computer lab, soccer field, cafeteria, and on and on. He said, "My goal is for the people to live here and work here. The bottom line is to get the people to help themselves."

She was thrilled with the vision, and if her children could be a part of that, then she would be more than happy. Willem supported her buy giving her some school supplies and a few books for the kids to use. This support continued on a regular basis during the spring.

In June of 1999, they made the public announcement of the new school's opening and held registration for the school. Parents came with their kids, and they were dressed in their Sunday best; these parents were proud to say that their children would be going to school. Beth started with the nineteen children from the previous school and built around them, adding sixty-nine other students for a total of eighty-eight. They recorded each student's name, age, parent's name, and the grade they would be in. Each student had their photograph taken and received a brand new school uniform to wear on the first day of school. These eighty-eight students were now designated as the select attendees of the new mountain school.

Raising Support

Roger and Lori Stroup visited Willem and offered to help get the project off the ground. Beth and Lori assigned each student a number and placed the student's name, number, and picture on a card for a student sponsorship program. With the cards in hand, and a plan in mind, Willem and Beth headed to visit Lori and Roger in the States to raise support saying, "These are our students who will be attending our new school!"

With hearts full of joy they shared their vision with friends and churches anywhere they could. However, MTM had no building. They had no teachers. They had no principal or any administration staff. They had no school supplies. But they had eighty-eight energetic and expectant students. Despite their shortcomings, they had hope and a plan. As Beth says, "That's just how Willem works. God takes people like that and uses them as they step out in faith."

The vision of the school and church on the mountainside was clear as Willem and Beth shared their hearts to church after church in Indiana. After each service, interested individuals would come to the back of the church and meet and excitedly share with Willem and Beth. A number of visionary sponsors stepped up to the new challenge. Gramothe's first student was a boy named Fritzner Jean. He was born on September 11, 1990 and was nine years old when he was able to start first grade. Nancy Gangwer, a longtime friend of Willem and Beth's from Hope Missions, sponsored him. Ten years later, he is a proud high school student and will be graduating with his class soon. After sharing the story countless times and presenting the idea of sponsoring students to groups and churches all over Indiana, Willem and Beth's confidence rose as sponsors joined their efforts. In August, with $7,000 in their pockets and a list of sponsors who pledged to send regular checks, Willem and Beth headed back home to Haiti to start the school and church.

Construction Begins

When construction started, there was absolutely nothing on the mountain except for fields and a few scattered shanties. No mission teams had visited the village, and nobody except a few brave sponsors had knowledge of the tremendous challenge that lay ahead. Mde Anisco Romelius was a matron of Haiti born on July 9, 1922. She lived her whole life in Gramothe and happily offered to give a parcel of her land to Willem for the church. Willem respectfully said, "Thank you, but no. We need to buy it from you." This was a relatively flat area of the mountainside, but the ground would require a significant amount of leveling before a foundation could be set.

After Willem arranged MTM's purchase of the property, he marked out the footprint for the new building with the whole village looking on. The work crew was made up entirely of the men, women, and children from the village. This building was going to be built by the people of Gramothe for the people of Gramothe. On Wednesday morning, October 6, 1999, with the vision of a church to worship in and a school for their children, the inspired crowd dove in with picks and shovels—the ground breaking of the church and school had begun.

Everyone had a job to do. Men swung pickaxes and shovels, little children carried blocks on their heads, and women helped with just about everything. The work crew had many hands but the work was not light. They heaved into the ground and worked to level the site, breaking up the rock and dirt, and setting it on the downhill side to create a flat site for a twenty-by-sixty-foot foundation, with a few feet of margin around it on all sides.

During the 1995 U.S. occupation, the army brought in loads of supplies including vehicles like a white half-ton Chevy truck that Willem bought after the soldiers departed. The payload bay had benches that the soldiers would sit on, and it was useful for hauling construction materials up the mountain. He bought twelve-foot long, rough-hewn lumber for building the rafters and benches. He planned to store them at to his house, but on the first trip, as he approached the house, the wood slipped from the truck—the weight of the boards was too much for the truck's tailgate. Nobody was hurt, and they quickly learned the limitations of the truck. After that they employed six young boys from the village to haul the boards up the mountain one by one. Each time a boy reached the house, Beth gave him an orange to eat before he set off with another board.

Willem bought concrete in eighty-pound bags and many truckloads of sand, and hauled it up the hill, one load at a time. A properly designed concrete mixture will possess the desired workability for the fresh concrete, and the required durability and strength for the hardened concrete. An ideal American mix is about 10 to 15 percent cement, 60 to 75 percent aggregate, and 15 to 20 percent water. The mixture is done with careful measurement and specialized equipment. It's a paradox that concrete with too much water at mixing is prone to cracking, but concrete without water at curing will also crack; skill is essential to get a good result. However, on a remote mountainside in Haiti, working without a mixing truck, a portable cement mixer, or even a wheelbarrow, the men created a cement mixing area and mixed one shovelful of concrete with three shovelfuls of sand, and added water carefully, mixing it on the ground with a shovel. With the mix dull in appearance, it was poured it into block-making molds to make cinder blocks for the walls.

Pouring the Foundation

To pour the concrete for the floor, they needed to have a large number of people working and mixing materials at the same time allowing for one continuous pour that would yield a solid concrete footing. The foundation was outlined with wooden boards, reinforced with rebar, and separators were placed to allow for expansion.

On the day of the pour, the women in the village came with their five-gallon buckets early in the morning. A long line of white buckets traveled on the heads of the hard-working women all day long as they walked up and down the mountain. Even the girls joined in bringing hundreds of gallons of water up the long, winding road. The men prepared a large mix of concrete and transferred the material from the mixing area to the building's base in small plastic buckets. Young boys helped carry the buckets over and poured the mix to form the foundation. After a long day of mixing, pouring, hiking, and smoothing, they sat under a shade tree and rested from their labor.

Before the work could proceed to the next step, each square foot of the structure had to undergo an inspection by the master worker, Willem. Amazingly, over the years, the Gramothe concrete crew has built over a dozen buildings mixing concrete in this manner without any significant structural weakness. With their rebar reinforcement, the buildings have resisted physical damage despite the running feet of thousands of children, the dragging and dropping of tables, chairs, and all sorts of musical and medical equipment, as well as the unrelenting forces of nature that include hurricane force winds and a earthquake that measured 7.0 on the Richter scale.

Final Touches

After the floor had cured, the walls were built using cinder blocks made at the site. Each wall's position was designated by a string of twine tied between a pair of sticks mounted in the dirt just beyond the foundation. With the walls true and corners set at ninety degrees, the door was framed and window sites left open. The windows were actually three-foot-square steel doors placed in a normal window position that swung open to let natural light in and swung closed to securely lock the building. This worked very well as the natural light is adequate for a classroom or sanctuary, and the soffits on the roof prevent the rain from cascading indoors. Only when the storms are heavy are the windows closed and students are dismissed from school early.

On Friday, October 22, the roof was installed. A classic front-gable plan was chosen. This simple design is inexpensive and easy to build. It effectively sheds water, allows for good ventilation, and provides the adequate ceiling space. The wooden roof trusses were built and installed in just two days. Then the stainless-steel sheet metal was nailed to place. No painting was necessary since it can be left to weather naturally, and the stainless steel panels refuse to rust.

On Saturday, October 30, the awning was constructed. The entryway gave character to the simple building, and an entrance point where people would pass through into a chamber where numerous lives would be changed forever. As the finishing touches were made to the building, the benches were being fabricated just outside. The benches were to serve many functions in the coming years. They were pews for the church, group desks for the school children, waiting-room sofas for patients in the medical clinic, and beds for an occasional villager needing a place to sleep.

Meanwhile, during the construction, Willem had been busy finding Christian teachers for his new school. With unemployment sky high in the region, it wasn't hard to find people who wanted the job. It was a little harder to find individuals with appropriate credentials to teach, but plenty of men and women stepped forward for the opportunity to hold these jobs. He interviewed and hired men and women for teacher positions. They were required to attend an orientation meeting where Willem trained them in the basics of how the school would be organized and run on a day-to-day basis. He gave them a modest budget and went with them to purchase their supplies for the first few weeks of school.

The fall of 1999 was a very active hurricane season, but, amazingly, construction was not delayed a single day due to weather while storms raged before they began and shortly after they completed the project. Three and a half weeks of labor had resulted in a solid concrete building. The entryway was completed on Saturday, and the following morning they held a Sunday morning celebratory worship service. Tired men, women, and children who were truly thankful for their new building attended the service. The music was simple, singing in traditional island style, and they gave God all the credit for their new church. Mde Romelius cried during the church service. Afterward, she approached Willem and said, "Now I can die in peace because we have a church in Gramothe."

School is in Session

On Monday November 1, 1999, the building was complete and the first classes of Gramothe Elementary School commenced.

Eighty-eight students arrived for their first day of class in the new school. Mothers and fathers arrived with their children attending them right up to the front door. Proudly wearing their turquoise pants and white shirts, the kids understood the significance of this great opportunity they had. Teachers organized the children into six classes, and after a little orientation and covering some of the rules, school was in session.

With kindergarteners and sixth graders all together, yet having quite different needs, teaching was a continual challenge. They functioned much like a traditional one-room schoolhouse, with students in many grades all-together in one large room. During the course of a day, they were grouped together for some activities and separated for others.

After a few weeks, Willem installed a pole at the front of the building and they raised the Haitian flag at the beginning of school, which started promptly at eight o'clock every day. The vast majority of the students had never been to school before and had no idea what was expected of them. Discipline was of the utmost importance, and teaching children to arrive punctually, to sit in class, and to participate in class recitations and songs all took some time. Eventually, the Gramothe School became known as a sharp, well-run school with children of promise.

By the beginning of December, the rainy season continued to bring inclement weather, and Hurricane Lenny, a category four hurricane that killed seventeen people on the tropical islands, had interrupted the warm tropical days. Despite the school being closed for several days, efforts were made to continue with life as normal in this village with a new bustling school. Teachers got used to the new routines, and students learned to look forward to recess.

The school taught primarily in French but also used Haitian Creole. Since French is the national language, any business of importance is done in French. While the children know Creole as the language they grew up with, they also need to be taught to read and write the French language for them to have a chance to advance.

In December, the school prepared for a Christmas program for the students. The students practiced their skits and learned Christmas songs. When the big day arrived, their parents were in attendance as the children put on a performance that made them proud. Each child received a shoebox full of gifts that had been donated by the church of one of the children's sponsors. The shoeboxes were distributed equally, and every child in the school received something for Christmas that year.

More Room

While the school continued to be held in the church, construction on more classrooms started right away. Willem and Beth put together a fund-raising campaign that raised $3,000 for classrooms. They leveled an area across from the front door of the church and built a small classroom that later became the principal's office. They continued this process of extending the construction and after a few years, when the classrooms were complete through sixth grade; no more classes were held in the church. One of the last buildings built was the larger building up the hill at the top of the other school buildings for the preschoolers.

The move to the new classrooms was done in stages. The first group to be sectioned out was the kindergarten class because they were the loudest. When they made the move, the kindergarteners loved their new home, and the rest of the classes appreciated the relative quiet in the church building. However, before the students were able to move in, a medical clinic was held in their designated space for a week. There was a group of doctors and nurses who came to visit MTM and provide medical care. They had previously set up clinics outside, but with a room built, the patients would be seen with some shelter, and it was easier to ensure privacy for patients. The school was cancelled for the week. This clinic would have caused a significant disruption of the school if it weren't for the graciousness and flexibility of the villagers who needed medical attention as much as they desired a quality education for their children.

After the one-week stay of the medical team, the class made their transition to their quiet new room and filled it with the type of cheers that can only come from a fun-loving group of kindergarteners. Over the next couple of years, they would donate their room to medical clinics multiple times until the medical building was constructed.

Growing Up

Each year, one grade level was added to the school, which allowed the students in the most senior grade level to continue with their education the following year. The new conservatively sized buildings were built up the hillside. They also added a pre-school, for kids three- to five-years-old to allow children to discover and explore freely at the early stages of cognitive development. These kids had their own yellow-and-blue uniforms, and received love and instruction each day that prepared them to enter kindergarten.

The school was started with the oldest students in the sixth grade. A few students who started in the sixth grade graduated to the seventh grade before the Gramothe School offered that level of studies. These students were sent to nearby schools, and MTM began the process of outsourcing their education until the higher-grade levels were complete. This process has continued and all of the students who began with Gramothe School have been supported throughout their education.

The first eighty-eight students were only from the village of Gramothe, and families were limited to one or two students per family. However, as the school grew, space opened up and more and more children from the village were attending school. Registration needed to be monitored carefully, and in the fourth year of the school, MTM required that each child have a birth certificate at registration. This was quite a stretch for many families who rarely made it out of the village. Many Haitians don't have a birth certificate; they do not know their birthday or even their age. As Willem explained, "Their worries are related to finding their next meal, not paperwork and dates." Willem then smiled and said, "But they don't get depressed when they turn forty because they don't know it if they just turned forty!"

MTM helped numerous families obtain birth certificates for their kids with legal registration at the magistrate (the Haitian version of city hall). Insisting on the legal paperwork was well worth the effort. Eventually, every child in the village was registered both with the Gramothe School and with the local government. By the school's fifth year, registration was opened up to select students from the surrounding villages. Students from as far as Belot, Kenscoff, Fercy, and Boucan (one of the poorest villages in the region) would come to school every day either making the two-hour walk or taking a tap-tap the majority of the way and walking the final two miles to Gramothe.

Eventually, school registration required both a birth certificate and immunization record. This was coordinated with the efforts of the medical teams who provided the shots. The immunization requirement is another step to a healthy and well-educated student population.

The Haitian school system is slightly different from the American system. Primarie (elementary school) is from kindergarten through the sixth grade. After sixth grade, the students must pass a government exam in order to advance to the seventh grade. The students prepare all year long for this exam, and the government sets the date and tells the students when and where to take the exam. They assign students in different schools for the exams by alphabetical order. Passing allows advancement, and failure generally means repeating the grade level. Secondaire (high school) is seventh through thirteenth grade. After the ninth grade students are required to pass another exam called the brevet to move up to the tenth grade. Then the exam called the retho allows passage to the thirteenth grade level.

The thirteenth grade is called the philo year (philosophy). The level of instruction is similar to the first year at a community college. Students at this level are required to write papers about three to five pages long every week. Additional large papers are assigned at the end of each trimester, and they are written in French and in English. Students graduate fluent in French and with knowledge of English.

The first year the students at the Gramothe School took the government exams, they had a 100 percent pass rate. Subsequent years showed excellent pass rates as well. Students occasionally struggle with the exams because of attendance issues. Since many of the students are the first in the history of their family to ever attend school, and the parents do not always place adequate emphasis on consistent attendance; some will occasionally pull their kids out of class for a few weeks or months for help with harvesting their crops. If the students miss even a little of the school year, they will certainly have difficulty passing the tests.

Dumay

As the school grew, MTM as an organization was progressing in a number of dimensions simultaneously. The church made progress by leaps and bounds. After a few years of working together, Gramothe was emerging as a place where every person had a job, farms were prosperous, and education was available to every child. Progress was taking place quickly, and the gospel of Jesus Christ was being proclaimed from the church regularly.

Willem had seen firsthand that many pastors and missionaries grow weary from the service to which they had dedicated their lives. He searched for a way to serve them and wanted to create a retreat center to bring pastors and families in for rest and a time of refreshing. A ten-acre plot of land in the village of Dumay that was flat and undeveloped (rare properties in the mountainous country) was available.

Similar to Gramothe's beginnings, Dumay was littered with voodoo temples, and the majority of the people were unemployed and uneducated. Willem said, "There were voodoo temples all over the place—at least ten in the village." Some were simple huts with thatched walls and a thatched roof; others were concrete buildings with symbols of St. Peter and other, mainly Catholic, figures painted on the outside. Willem continued, "They had lots of rich soil and beautiful flat land, with water running from the river nearby that they could use for irrigation, but they didn't farm. This is a good example of how the demon spirits keep you in the bondage of poverty, so you can't see farther than your nose."

The area was hot and humid. La Riverie de la Grise separated the village from the nearby town. It was the universal water source, for washing, watering the animals, and anything else; there was no source of clean drinking water. The owner of the property in Dumay knew what Willem had done in Gramothe and offered to sell the land to MTM at a discounted price with the understanding that he would also build a school, which was desperately needed in the village.

When he looked at Dumay, Willem saw more than just a hot and dusty village with voodoo temples and a big river; he saw possibilities. Along with a school and a church, he could dig a well and irrigate the fields for prosperous farms. A clinic could serve the people's medical needs. But most of all, this could be a place for the pastors' retreat center that he wanted.

Willem purchased the land and immediately went to work building a school. Three buildings of cinder block and concrete were erected to house the preschool and elementary school. They built a cafeteria, dug a well, and became the only functioning school in the village. The student sponsorship program was expanded to include students in the new Dumay schools.

However, the process of building the school was hard on everybody. On a typical day it would be 72 degrees up in the mountains in Gramothe, but it could easily reach 100 to 110 degrees in the valley of Dumay. At one point, a construction team was helping install the roof on the school buildings. The heat was unbearable, and there wasn't even a slight breeze to cool them down. Perched on top of the steel framework, one of the team members became lightheaded and almost passed out because of the heat. He took shelter in the shade, and with a little water and rest and he was fine. This incident, however, made Willem rethink the possibility of holding a pastor's retreat center at that location. With the heat consistently unbearable for those not accustomed to it, it might not be the best place to host missionaries and pastors. The school continues to make a difference in hundreds of children's lives and the vision continues as one grade level is added per year until the high school is complete.

Parent-Teacher Meetings

Parents play an important role in the school, and parent-teacher meetings are held twice a year. Beth commented about the meetings saying, "They are very well-attended, and people come on time." She laughed out loud since so few things in the Haitian culture are actually punctual. The meetings were held in the church, and essentially all the parents attend to hear the teachers and administrators provide important information and to share their input, which was then taken into consideration by the administration. For example, the school added a cafeteria in 2004 and provides students with a free hot meal each day. At a parent-teacher meeting, parents expressed their wish that children pay for the meals. They came up with amount of three Haitian cents a day (about 0.3 cents U.S.). These parents saw the daily meals as another teaching opportunity and wanted their kids to be responsible with money. This policy was instituted and remains in place.

Nene Pierre, was a native of Gramothe and a voodoo priest. Nene saw what Willem was doing in the village with the church and school, and when the school opened, he knew this was a great opportunity for his children to have an education. So, while he retained his position as a voodoo priest, he also wanted his children to attend the new Christian school. When the school opened, he registered his two kids and dutifully sent them on time every day. Since the students are also required to attend church every Sunday, Nene's kids followed suit and became regular church attendees. Over the years, Nene's kids became well versed in biblical teaching and shared the gospel of Jesus Christ with their father. After some time, Nene attended church with his kids and eventually gave his heart to Jesus Christ, giving up voodoo entirely. For the last several years he has been active in the church and holds a steady job as a member of Willem's work crew that builds roads, walls, and buildings for MTM.

School Visitors

Sponsors and working teams visit Gramothe on a regular basis. The kids are quite used to seeing the white faces of foreigners looking inquisitively at them as they wind their way up the mountain in the back of a truck. On a medical mission trip in 2004, sixteen visitors rode up to the clinic. Each team member had a camera, and when they arrived, the clicking begins. Individual pictures of the team members, group pictures of the whole team, as well as pictures of the church, school, and especially the students were continuous. After a little acclimation, the team set to their task for the day and work begins. During lunch break the kids at the school are always somehow involved. Some of the team members played soccer with the kids, some had learned enough Haitian Creole to sit and chat with the kids, and some just held the little ones on their laps.

Willem found a time at the end of a lunch break on the third day of the team's clinic to take the team on a tour. With a small entourage following close behind him, he retold the story of how MTM started, as he crossed between kids playing soccer. Heading up the elementary school's steps he told about the playground and the preschool, and took extra time to introduce the school's principal to the team.

Willem entered a room full of children for the team to see a class in session. He spoke a few words to the teacher and then looked over the class. The second graders were absolutely still and sat with their feet dangling off the benches, toes barely touching the cement floor. They were packed shoulder to shoulder like sardines. Their papers lay on the desks before them, and pencils were either in their hands or on the desks. The work would have to wait; now it was time to sing. Willem stepped forward and slowly and rhythmically sang out, "En, dez, twa."

The students took their cue and sang out in unison a beautiful Haitian Creole version of "This Is the Day That the Lord Has Made." Not just a few lines but the entire song. A few kids swung back and forth, and attracted the attention of the visiting crowd; some kids attempted to hide behind their neighbors and avoided all eye contact, but most faithfully sang and smiled. The boys' closely trimmed haircuts and the girls' hairpins framed their perfect smiles. When the performance ended, the team applauded and Willem spent a couple of minutes with the teacher as the team chatted with the students in the front row.

The tour continued to see the preschool that recently had received a beautiful tile floor. As the team became educated about and impressed with the progress the school has made, many of them asked questions. Some of the questions were:

o   Before this school was here, what did these children do?
o   What sports to the children play?
o   How can they balance buckets on their heads like that?

Willem took time with each of these questions and gave answers that he's given hundreds of times before to other teams. He responded with clarity and respect, giving time to each person. A six-year-old girl, the daughter of one of the nurses on the team, raised her hand and asked Willem where the library was. Willem sat down on a chair, pulled her up on his lap, and said, "We're still working on that one. We don't have one yet, but we hope to soon."

Not only did they ask questions, many people came with suggestions. Visitors related to how their schools back home did things and suggested various things:

o   A larger administration staff with secretaries to handle the school's paperwork and assistants for the teachers.
o   Carpet in the rooms to keep the noise down.
o   If you had more space, the kids don't have to sit shoulder to shoulder in their desks.
o   You need a computer lab to teach computer skills to the children.

Willem remained gracious and accepted the advice from each and every visitor. The simple fact of the matter was that schools in Haiti are different from schools in the United States. The administrative staff is a skeleton crew, but they keep the school running; while a larger staff would be nice, controlling cost is important. Carpet is not practical in this setting because when it rains, mud is tracked everywhere and cleaning would be a nightmare. Haitian kids don't mind sitting shoulder to shoulder because they don't have the same personal space issues that Americans have. But Willem didn't say any of these things, he just acknowledged their counsel and remarked on where they've been as a school and outlined the next classrooms to be built. Suggestions are good, in fact many of the things that have happened at MTM are the result of various suggestions, however, there is a sifting process in understanding which are viable and which are not.

Computer Lab

Beth Jones had visited MTM several times and was a faithful student sponsor. When she heard about a computer upgrade that was taking place at Southwest Allen County Schools, where she worked, her ears perked up. She inquired, "What's going to happen to all the old computers?" When she heard that they were heading to the landfill, Beth immediately asked to collect them and donate them to the Gramothe School. She took the computers, which had plenty of life still in them, and arranged for them to be shipped to MTM.

A team of computer guys went down for a week to set up a classroom with the computers. When they arrived, the room that they were to use was almost complete, with the floor tile laid on their first day. The team ran wire from the generator and constructed a unique battery backup system that allows every computer to run off an individual battery. This regulated the power and gave protection to the sensitive equipment. On the second day, they painted the room, hauled the computers up to the school, and began to set them up. Out of the twelve that were donated, ten made it without any traumatic damage in transit, they set aside the rest to be used for replacement parts. They installed the computers as a complete teaching system, where the teacher's computer had access to each of the other units. A printer was installed, and plenty of paper and toner were stored in a cabinet underneath it. They loaded each station with the programs that they would need and set up a bootable ghost image so that if the programming began to have errors, as is common with student computers, they could get it back to its appropriate settings by simply inserting a CD into the drive.

Beth's daughter, Lisa, had been attending Indiana University-Purdue University at Fort Wayne at the time. She helped with the set up, and when she turned on the first terminal, she looked behind her and saw a crowd of smiling faces. The kids saw the shining image from the monitor and thought that it was a television. Some of them had seen televisions in the city, but nobody had seen a computer. She showed them what it was, and as she typed on the keyboard, they were mesmerized.

Lisa graciously offered to take a semester off from college to be the computer teacher for the school. For the next five months, she taught math, spelling, English, and basic computer skills to the kids. Students would rotate through the computer room as a part of their regular curriculum. After school, the computer room offered something extra for the talented students who were doing well in their regular classes. Lisa stayed late every afternoon for these students and it functioned as a gifted and talented program. Beth and Lisa helped pioneer a great addition to the Gramothe School. When she completed her semester, her work was taken over by Haitian computer lab teacher.

High School

As the school matured and added buildings, the Gramothe Elementary School took on the appearance of a traditional school and was meeting the needs of the children. As the students graduated from elementary school, however, their needs changed as they approached high school. Adding additional classrooms to the existing school wouldn't be appropriate. They needed a facility of their own. Willem selected the site for the high school and bought the land. However, the slope was steeper than anything he had ever built on before, and he was concerned about the structural integrity of the mountain. He decided that he needed to hire a specific type of engineer with geological experience and get the advice of a contractor before proceeding.

In September 2004, Ron Ediger was visiting Haiti to help another organization build a little church in a village north of Port-au-Prince. He was told that the cost would be about $20,000. They had half of the cost covered, and Ron volunteered to cover the remainder and went down with a small team to see the project in action. They left on a Monday morning and stayed in a hotel in Port-au-Prince. Before they made it to the village the team went to the various local supply stores to price the materials for the project. It turned out to be about half of the original estimate, which was great news, but it caused Ron to wonder why he was there. If his donation was not needed, what would he do?

The following day, Hurricane Ivan, the tenth most intense Atlantic hurricane ever recorded, swept through the island country with a terrible force. It was a category five storm with winds reaching 165 miles an hour. Low-lying areas suffered massive flooding, and countless Haitians were drowned. The village that Ron was heading for was right in the middle of the affected area.

Their trip was in jeopardy of being cut short because the roads had flooded out, and they simply couldn't get to their destination. Ron simply prayed, "God, show me beyond the shadow of a doubt why I'm here." One of their local contacts gave Ron Willem's phone number and explained that Willem was building a ministry up in the mountains not far from Port-au-Prince. After a short phone call, Willem sent one of his men in a car to bring the team up for a visit.

Ron said, "When we got there, Willem took us from his home up to the village and showed us around. He told us the story of the five voodoo temples that had been there, and how the church and school has changed everything. We heard the story of the clean water that the village now has and saw the clinic in action. I looked at the architect of the ministry and asked, 'What's next?'"

Willem replied, "I need a high school. We have the land, and the students will be finishing elementary school next spring, so we need to build the high school very soon. In order to build it, first I need a geotechnical engineer. And once I get the money, we'll start building."

Ron looked at Willem and grinned, "Well, I'm a contractor, and one of the guys on our team is a geotechnical engineer!" God's grace provided the people Willem needed right there in the village at the right time.

That day, Ron's team went to work on the hillside. Willem outlined the needs for the school, and the team evaluated the soil and rock on the slope and began the series of calculations required for planning such a building. They started to put their thoughts together and designed a grand arcing building in the shape of Hoover Dam with classrooms that terraced down the mountain. This would provide the structure they needed and stability on the steep hillside. The following day, Willem's construction team headed to the site with shovels and pickaxes and began the foundation for the school.

Ron remembered, "When I looked over the land where the high school would be built, a soft, still voice in my heart said, 'Ron, this is why you are here.' At that point, I knew without a shadow of a doubt why we were there."

After a few more days of evaluation, planning, and calculating, the team headed back home. Ron said, "When I got home, one of my cousins came over, and I told him the story of what was happening in Gramothe. Right then and there, he pulled out his checkbook and wrote a check for $20,000. From then on, money has rolled in from a variety of sources. At one point, I put in $3,500 and the next day a donation for $35,000 came in. The high school has become a reality, and I was only used as a vessel."

Construction of this project was long and hard because the building was significantly larger than any previous classroom building. After four months of construction, with the first day of school quickly approaching, the foundation was in place, the three floors were framed up, and space was created for nine classrooms The first three classrooms were completed just before the first day of school. The structure had rebar emanating from every corner and pillar, the balconies overlooking the future classrooms below had yet to be finished, but the three classrooms were there for the students, and the high school opened on time.

Viergina and Oliver

Viergina had been in Gramothe Elementary School for several years and was looking forward to being a part of the new Gramothe High School. She was the oldest of five children; her two younger brothers attended the elementary school, and her four-year-old sister was in the preschool. Her baby brother, Oliver, was an active two-year-old and a handful for Viergina's mother. In the spring, when time came to register kids for the following school year, Viergina's brothers and sister came with their paperwork and signed up for school, but Viergina did not. Her parents needed her at home to help with Oliver, and they determined that she would not go to high school.

When the school's principal, Bermmane, saw this, he approached Willem about the loss of a good student. Bermmane and Willem took a hike up to Viergina's home and met with her parents try to convince them to keep Viergina in school. As they stood outside the house, Willem discussed how important it is for Viergina to finish high school. While they wanted to, her parents needed her help at home so they could do their daily work in the field.

Willem reached down and picked up the smiling Oliver and held him on his hip. Oliver smiled at him, and Willem smiled back; turning to the parents and said, "Why don't we put Oliver in preschool a little early, and then Viergina can finish her education." Viergina beamed with delight! Her parents hugged Willem in celebration.

Bermmane began thinking about all the ramifications of this new school policy. He looked down at the ground and considered the problems ahead. He would need another teacher for two-year-olds and more space. Where would he put all the kids? How many two-year-olds would they accept? Is this becoming a day care? He stopped for a moment and looked at Viergina's smiling face. Resolved to let her continue her education, he smiled back at Willem, and acccpted the challenge. She would be in school and have a chance to complete her education and that's what they wanted.

Soon, when the first day of school came, Viergina walked down the mountain holding Oliver's hand and beaming with delight.

Sponsor Relationship

The school was made possible financially by the generosity of hundreds of people who participated in MTM's sponsorship program. Sponsors who commit to sponsoring students for $25 each month provide the funds necessary each month pay for the staff and supplies at the school. The sponsor's faithfulness to their children truly provides the education of a generation in a country that often has no hope. Once the cafeteria was in place, MTM was able to tell the sponsors that their support also provided a hot meal for their child every day. In many cases this was the only meal the children get each day. Uniforms and school supplies are also included for every student as well. The student sponsorship program makes all this possible.

A sponsor's giving is great, but when the child actually has a relationship with their sponsor, it brings a new level of understanding to the child. Willem was been known to come into a classroom with a letter in his hands from a sponsor. He would take the child by the hand, go to a quiet place, and read the letter to the child. He'll translate it and explain that the person who wrote the letter cares for them so much that they have paid for them to be able to go to school. Beth commented, "I think the greatest thing for the kids is they know that someone somewhere is there for them and has knowledge of them. Also when a sponsor writes to their student we do everything we can to make sure the sponsor gets a letter back."

In their letters, sponsors often ask questions like: What do you like to do after school? What is your favorite subject? Do you have any pets? Answering these questions in their return letters is a great opportunity for the children to learn creative writing skills and think independently. This is different from the rote system of learning that they often get in the classroom.

There are always some students who are not able to go to school. When a young man or woman starts first grade as a teenager, though they try, it is an insurmountable task to delay a full-time job and the pay that comes with it to finish their education. MTM has done its best to creatively help students who are determined to succeed.

One such student was Eddie Augustine, an energetic hard-working high school student who was known as the class clown. He was a cut up in class and lots of fun to be around, but he honestly didn't see himself in school for much longer. Looking at his future, Eddie explained to Willem that he aspired to become a tile boss, the Haitian term for a contractor who lays ceramic tile. This young man had been in the Gramothe School for nine years and was doing well, but had moved out on his own and needed a job. The job he aspired to has promise for a long-term career. He knew that he needed help to accomplish his goal, so he wrote a letter that MTM sent to his sponsor, Mrs. Chateau. (The students don't have the contact information of their sponsors.) In the letter he explained Eddie's situation in some detail and asked for help. Mr. and Mrs. Chateau were very understanding and not only supported Eddie's decision to become a tile boss, but they gladly donated money for him to get the tools of the trade. When the donation arrived, Willem bought Eddie a ceramic tile cutter and a level. Eddie lost no time in learning his new trade.

Since the high school Eddie had been attending was also under construction, he knew that tile work would be required in that very building. When it came time to lay tile in two new high school classrooms, the newly formed Gramothe Tile Crew was there and offered to do the job! Willem gladly gave the entrepreneur the job and was pleased to see former students Wismane Faustin, James Emile, and Bertrand Excellent who had left school before graduating among the crew. The young men worked hard and provided a good service to their previous school. Willem was delighted to see the quality of their work, and these young men continue to work installing tile all around the region.

Careers

Since the medical clinic has always been a part of MTM and bringing quality medical care to the village was an important component of bringing the gospel of Jesus Christ, the doctor's services were made available to all the students in the school. Every time a medical team was there, the students receive the attention and medications they require.

When the children are asked what they want to do when they grow up, many report that they want to be nurses or interpreters. Others say they want to be in construction. While many of the visitors had to raise money to cover the cost of airfare to come and serve, they are viewed by the villagers as being wealthy and successful. In a community where the majority of the foreigners who come to visit are either building something or are part of a medical team, these are the primary vocations that the kids see as role models. Time will tell what kind of variety of career choices the students at Gramothe will have.

Celebration

As Gramothe's ninth school year came to a close, Willem and Principal Bermmane prepared for a year-end party. These children rarely get to have a party and what better time than the last day of school to really celebrate? At minimal cost, the school rented a bounce house and a snow-cone machine, and cooked hot dogs for the kids. This was a party without precedence for the mountain village. None of the children had ever seen a snow cone before! With the ice shaving machine spinning round and round, the children were amazed and curious as to what would come of the red and blue liquids in those funny looking bottles on top of the box-shaped machine. Smiling faces crowded around the unusual contraption, and when the first student to receive a snow cone held it carefully, surprised by how cold it was in his hands. He licked it, his eyes brightened, and he shouted out the Creole version of "Oh, yummy!" The crowd of curious kids quickly formed a line and each was anxious for their chance to taste this wonderful treat. The bounce house was equally breathtaking for the kids. Despite no experience with it, the kids inherently knew exactly what to expect, and as soon as the squirrel fan filled the air mattress, a carnival was in full swing. Every child had a snow cone, hot dogs, and bounced and ate to their heart's content.

MTM's schools have grown to enroll approximately 1,500 students in 2009 with preschool classes one, two, and three, as well as Kindergarten through the eleventh grade. The schools have changed the outlook on life for a generation of children who now have a clear path to get an education; they also are blessed with burgeoning relationship with Jesus Christ. Soon, Gramothe High School will hold it's first ever graduation, which will be a tremendous celebration in the village and beyond. The graduates will have opportunities to work locally or in the cities. They will also be eligible for college or trade school. These boys and girls who were born on the side of a mountain are the future of their country. They will become the men and women who are lawyers, engineers, teachers, and politicians who will be leaders of Haiti in the years to come. Many will have the opportunity to travel and jobs will open up for them in other countries, but the message to them is clear: the students who are trained in Haiti are encouraged to stay in Haiti and be a blessing for their country.

Willem Charles brings a word of encouragement to his congregation in Gramothe, Haiti.

Beth Tyron came from a modest family in Terre Haute, Indiana. She pioneered a ministry to kids in the inner city, which provided valuable experience for her prior to working with children in Haiti.

Willem Charles and Beth Tyron were married on June 30, 1994 in a beautiful ceremony at Wahoo Bay Beach on the north shores of Haiti.

Sharon Johnson, Judy Tharpe, and Bob Johnson (from left to right). Bob and Sharon mentored Willem for a decade while he worked for them at Hope Missions Outreach in Haiti. Willem remembers them fondly and refers to Sharon saying, "She's like my mom." Judy Tharpe was also an American missionary who lovingly mentored Willem.

Willem interpreted for missionaries all over the Port-au-Prince region. Here he is interpreting on a makeshift stage for Gary Linton at the Mission of Hope complex in 1990.

Prior to 1999, Gramothe was primitive. They had very few job opportunities, five voodoo temples and no hope. Homes like this one made from pieced together scrap metal were all that many families had for shelter.

This was one of the few relatively flat areas of the mountainside. Willem insisted on buying it from a generous matron who wanted to help Willem build the church in the village. After further leveling, it became the site for MTM's first building.

On the day that the foundation for the church was poured, women and girls walked up and down the long winding road from the river to the construction site all day long bringing hundreds of gallons of water up to mix the concrete.

The roof for the church was installed using rough-hewn lumber purchased locally.

On Monday November 1, 1999, the building was complete after only three weeks of work. The entire village had been involved and their reward was a school for the children and a church for everyone.

The new school held a Christmas program in the church. The students practiced their skits and songs and performed for their parents. Afterward, each child received a shoebox full of gifts.

Nene Pierre was a voodoo priest native to Gramothe. Nene saw the school as a great opportunity for his children so he enrolled his two kids in the school. Over the years, his kids became well versed in Biblical teaching and shared the gospel of Jesus Christ with their father who eventually gave his heart to Jesus Christ and gave up his voodoo practice.

In 2004, after the voodoo priests had either left or joined the church, the voodoo drums were no longer heard in the valley. A steeple was generously donated and shipped to Gramothe. Willem installed it at the front of the new church building. The entire village and surrounding area can see the cross as it is lit up at night.

Lunch is served for the preschool children in the cafeteria at the school in Gramothe. The cafeteria comfortably seats over 200 children at a time.

Willem takes a few moments to read letters from sponsors to some of the elementary school kids in the Gramothe School.

Eddie Augustine (third from left) was an energetic student at Gramothe High School who worked with Willem and his sponsors to start a business installing ceramic tile. For his crew he recruited former students (from left to right), James Emile, Bertrand Excellent and Wismane Faustin who had previously dropped out of school and proudly pose here with Willem on the job site. They now form the Gramothe Tile Crew.

Bringing clean water from a spring in the mountains down into the village was an engineering feat that completely changed the village. Two inch black piping emerges from the base of the dam and delivers water from the fresh spring all the way down to the village. Free from the parasites and plentiful enough to irrigate their fields, the living water has changed the face of the village. This photo is one of three that are framed and mounted at the front of the Gramothe church.

Every square foot of the village, which is not too steep to be tilled, was cultivated. With the advent of the irrigation, the skillful farmers have transformed from raising one crop a year to four crops annually.

Construction has continued in Gramothe ever since the first building was built. Here, workers who have mixed a large amount of concrete are bringing it up a ladder to the roof bucket by bucket as they pour the roof as a number of classrooms are added to the school.

Willem is seated in front of Madam Stephen's home in the village. Mme. Stephen worked hard in the school and church as Willem's right hand since the beginning of MTM. She also ran a business growing and selling coffee using the profits to build her home which she completed in 2008.

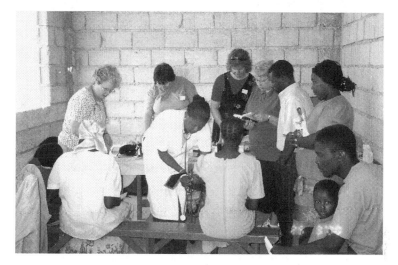

From the beginning MTM held medical clinics to minister to the physical needs of the people in the village and surrounding areas. This photo shows one of the early clinics held in the school building with the examination, treatment area as well as the pharmacy all together in the small kindergarten classroom.

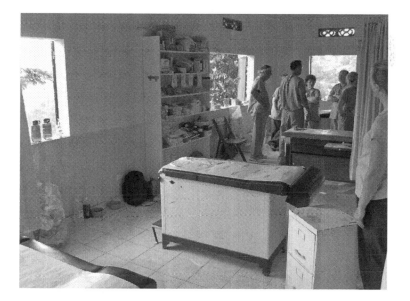

The construction of a separate clinic building allowed multiple treatment areas, which are shown here as the clinic is ready to open for the day. There are also separate rooms for waiting area, pharmacy, and administration.

Willem's back porch provides a clear view of the village as it overlooks the valley between Thomassin and Gramothe. Among his many activities, he has also managed to take guitar and piano lessons and plays along with the worship team in the Gramothe church.

Willem wrestling with his two sons.

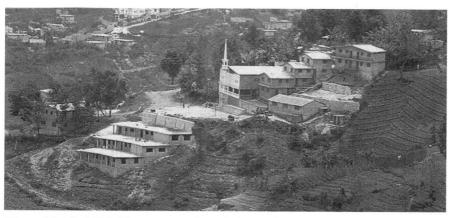

Since 1999, MTM has grown from being a dream in Willem's mind's eye, to being the source for economic, academic and spiritual development for Gramothe and the surrounding areas.

CHAPTER 7
THE CHURCH

And I tell you that you are Peter, and on this rock I will build my church, and the gates of Hades will not overcome it.

Matthew 16:18

The poverty-stricken tropical hillside a dozen miles southwest of Port-au-Prince seemed to be a thousand miles from anywhere until Willem Charles made the statement, "I'm going to build a church and a school here." With the collective energy of the entire village, they had poured in their labor to build the school knowing that the project included not only a school, but also a Christian church. Yet, most of the village was devoted to voodoo. Other than the two families in the village who had vowed to help him, the remaining villagers were firmly ingrained in their voodoo and would have no part of changing. Willem was well aware that they were only going to be moved by something that was going to change them for the better.

When Willem began the construction project, he invited his old friend Pastor Roger Stroup (who he knew from his previous work at Hope Mission Outreach) to visit them at their new ministry and planned to hold a revival meeting as soon as the school building was complete. He told Roger, "I want you to preach, and I'll interpret for you. Keep it simple and explain the gospel of Jesus Christ just as you've done thousands of times before."

Roger smiled at the opportunity to do the one thing he loved to do most. He recalled, "At that time, the villagers did not really know Willem. They knew who he was and what he said he would do there, but there had not been enough time for any real trust to build up yet." In fact, other that the three and a half weeks of working together building the solitary building on the mountain, they really hadn't had much interaction with this energetic young visionary since his days playing in the village as a child. Willem planned a crusade to be held in the village, just outside the new school building. Traditionally, Haitian crusades are held from Sunday to Sunday with meetings in the morning and each evening throughout the week. The gospel of Jesus Christ is delivered and practical life application points are presented all along the way. Willem had Pastor Roger put together a team to help with the music and scheduled the crusade for just after the opening of the school.

Construction of the school building was completed on Monday November 1, 1999. Teachers were hired, classes were called to order, and the school began operation. Willem had spent almost all of the MTM money that had been raised on the building and was dependent on the few donors who sponsored children to provide necessary funds to pay the teachers. While he had arranged for a crusade in the village, this would cost money and require a large place to hold it. Willem managed to construct an outdoor stage for the crusade with rented plywood and two- by-four boards from a local supplier in front of the school building.

The First Team

Pastor Roger and his three accompanying team members stepped off American Airlines flight 625 in the early afternoon and walked down the staircase to the Port-au-Prince tarmac. They were greeted with 92-degree sunshine and dense humidity. They walked inside past an accordion band and stood in line at the customs agent. After having their passports stamped, they found Willem standing next to the rotating luggage rack. Willem greeted his friend Roger, "So good to see you my friend. I can't wait to see what God will do through this crusade." Roger introduced his team: Bill, Brock, and Josh. They each received a warm welcome, and Willem helped them collect their baggage and had the team line up behind him as they went through the customs line with

their stack of suitcases. The agent in charge of customs was an old acquaintance of Willem's, and they shook hands in a friendly exchange. Willem explained that these men were with him for a crusade at a new ministry he had started. He was welcome to search their suitcases, as is their protocol. The agent opened one and gave a cursory look, then waved the men through.

The team exited the airport and headed to Willem's truck. In the process, each man was approached by dozens of "porters" who grabbed their bags and offered to help. These men who were seemingly attached to them were not employees of the airport but ambitious unemployed men who hung around the parking lot in hopes of helping people with their bags. They aggressively took over by grabbing the American's luggage and walking them through the parking lot, which was full of potholes and cracked concrete. Willem shouted out instructions in Creole to the porters and in English to the team as the now massive group headed across the parking lot to Willem's truck. They loaded a couple of guys in the front and the two more adventurous men rode in the back with the luggage. Willem addressed one of the porters and gave him some Haitian currency and the remaining porters continued to holler and plead as Willem exited the airport. They made the hour-long drive up to Thomassin forty-eight.

When the team arrived at Willem's house, they noticed it was considerably cooler, about seventy-two degrees and not as humid. Roger inquired, "How high are we?"

"Oh we're about 3,000 feet up from the ocean. Much nicer up here, don't you think?" Willem responded. They unloaded the truck, and Willem brought the team in the house. It didn't take long for the team to notice that the house was still under construction.[1] It's typical in Haiti to live in your house while it's being built and for Willem and Beth, this meant not only

1 Within a couple of years, Willem finished the home. He added the second floor and sleeping quarters to comfortably house twenty-four visitors. The home was equipped with electrical power and wireless Internet access. Teams may also keep in touch with their loved ones via e-mail or Skype. Many individuals brought movies for evening entertainment, and they form a family-friendly DVD collection that sits next to the television and DVD player. The kitchen has been equipped with all the modern facilities one would expect in an American kitchen and boasts a Haitian cook. Willem and his family now live in a separate home they built adjoining the property of the first home, which now has the sole purpose of being a guest house.

living in it, but also hosting teams in their unfinished home. The outside walls of the first floor were done, and the windows installed, but the staircase was a skeleton of boards. Not that there would be anything to visit on the second floor because above the first floor there was only rebar—a Haitian promise of future square feet. A pile of dry cement mix sat in the middle of the room, ready to be used for finishing touches soon. A bed sheet was hung over the doorways as temporary doors. The front of the house was for the guests and Willem, Beth, and their four-year-old son, Stephen, occupied the back bedroom. Borrowed steel bunk beds provided enough sleeping quarters for the team.

At Beth's request, the team had brought various household odds and ends, and she repaid her international shoppers. There was no electric power in the home, but Willem told the team of his plans for a generator and an inverter with a series of batteries so that power would be constant without interruption. But at the time, evening entertainment consisted of sitting around and sharing stories by flashlight.

After orientation to the home and a nice meal, Willem stood comfortably in his living room surrounded by the volunteers on MTM's first mission team. He addressed the group, "Welcome to our home. We are so glad that you have come all this way down to serve God in Haiti with us. I know you could have gone a lot of different places and done a lot of different things with your time, so I appreciate that you have given of your time to be here. When you go to various places in Haiti you'll see lots of people begging and asking you for things as you walk by. You certainly saw that already at the airport. That's not how it will be here at Mountain Top Ministries. We want our people to have pride in themselves and work for their income not beg from visitors. In order to make this happen, we have some rules we ask you, as a team, to follow. First of all never give out your address to anyone. If you're working with an interpreter all week long and have a friendship with them, they may ask you for your home or e-mail address. If you give out your address, they will contact you with a sad story and ask you for money. Or they may

manage to get to the Miami Airport and send you a message saying, 'I'm here please come and get me!' You see, you'll be the only contact they have in the States, and they will assume that you can pick them up at the drop of a hat. They don't understand that you live a thousand miles away from Miami. So please, do not give out your address. If anybody asks you for your contact information and presses you, tell them to see Mr. Willem. They know the rules and just telling them to talk to me will solve the problem.

"Secondly, don't give anybody anything while you are here. Giving food or candy or money is not the best way to help. If you do that, then the next team that comes down here will be bombarded with people asking them for things. If people press you for money or a gift, tell them to see Mr. Willem and that will solve it. We want our people to be successful and hard working. The interpreters are paid, and it's not for you to tip them extra. If they do a great job and want extra work for extra money, let me know, and I'll provide that work for them.

"Now, the most important thing is that you guys realize the importance of the work you will be doing here. The men and women in this village have built a school because they believe in the promise of education for their children. They also know that along with a school comes a church, but they don't know about a healthy church. They've never seen what God's love, when expressed from one member of the congregation to another can look like. They don't know God, and certainly have never heard about Jesus. You guys are here on the tip of the spear to make a difference in their lives. I want you to do your best to show them Jesus while you are here as our guests." Willem then turned the floor over to Beth who concluded with a few comments about the meal plans, Haitian plumbing intricacies, and where to find the bottled water.

The crusade was set to begin that evening, so Bill and Roger trekked over to the village to see the setup. Willem had arranged for a Haitian worship team to come and lead singing. The musicians brought their guitars and drums and set up on the provisional stage to warm up. A constant creaking sound became background noise as the plywood tested the pullout strength of

the reused nails in the platform. A small generator that sat only a few yards away, adding to the background white noise powered the simple sound system.

Bill said, "We arrived during worship. It was *National Geographic!* Here we are overlooking a lush, green mountain of tropical plants and trees. The people are all black, singing unfamiliar 'island' songs in a foreign language. They're all dressed like Americans except just once in a while there will be something just a little off, like a lady wearing a formal dress with plastic sandals."

Roger recalled, "While the plywood was rickety, and I was worried about how stable the stage was. I preached each night and Willem interpreted for me. It was amazing how receptive the people were. There were between 150 to 200 people there, and they listened intently." The worship leader was very energetic, started off the meeting, and kept the ball rolling nicely. The keyboard and guitarist played island style worship with a Caribbean flare while the people sang and danced.

After the time of worship, Roger took the podium and a taught lesson on David and Goliath; he skillfully wove this story into a discussion about Jesus. The people had never heard the classic Old Testament story before, and they loved it. After he was done, the crowd became very animated. They kept saying the name Jesus as they discussed the story amongst themselves. It was a message that many of the people had never heard before and the response was terrific. When the altar call was given that night, twenty-five people came forward and gave their hearts to the Lord that night.

The following day, Bill and Roger took a tour of the village of Gramothe early in the day. They walked up the mountain to the school and went further up into an area that had a number of small homes bunched together. They began chatting with an older woman who sat outside of her smokehouse shelling beans as smoke poured out the door. The smokehouse was nothing more than a collection of five-foot-by-five-foot corrugated steel panels supported by sticks with a small wood fire inside. Through an interpreter, Roger shared the story of who Jesus was with her. She was honest and calmly stated that she did not have Jesus in

her heart. They encouraged her to come to the meetings that would be held each evening.

That night the service was terrific, and Roger saw his new friend who had been shelling beans and greeted her warmly. During the worship, the leader worked up the people into a frenzied dance. The hard packed dirt was stirred up and sent up a giant cloud of thick dust into the air. When this happened the people scattered leaving a giant hole in the middle of the crowd until the dust cleared. This happened three times through the worship experience. Afterward, Roger gave a sermon on the eternally unchanging God. He pulled a Mr. Potato Head toy out of his backpack and used it as an illustration. Roger explained that there is a Buddhist temple in Asia where you can "design" your own God with blue eyes, blonde hair, and a tan. Just like a Mr. Potato Head. But the God of the Bible is the creator of the world, and he does not change, no matter what we think he should or should not be. The people were not only amused by the example, but they were fed by the rich yet simple message.

After the service concluded at about nine o'clock in the evening, they headed back to Willem's home. The long road down the mountain gave them time to think about what had happened and to pray that God would continue to touch the people with the clear message of the gospel. Back at the house, they ate dinner and relaxed for a bit before going to bed. Late at night, they could hear the constant beating of voodoo drums, a feature of most of Haiti.

On the third day, Bill remembered, "The voodoo drums started up again after the service, which lead me to believe that the crowd celebrating voodoo were the same people who were at the service." The walk home was eventful, "This time we took another way from before, and we had to literally climb a up a rock face at a seventy-five degree angle in the dark. The path was shaded from the moon, which was extremely bright there. You don't need a flashlight to see anything. You could plainly see a mile away with out squinting. It was just amazing. And the stars were brighter and clearer than I'd ever seen before. What a retreat!"

Roger recalled, "I preached my heart out every night, and we had altar calls. By the end of the week a total of seventy-seven

people had come forward and given their hearts to Jesus Christ."
One of the men who came forward was a voodoo priest. He
came humbly to the front of the crowd. Willem recognized him
and went to speak with him. When it became clear that he had
come forward to give his life to Christ and not for another more
nefarious reason, Roger and Willem walked him through the
process of devoting his life to Jesus Christ. Willem spent some
time with him and instructed him on the depth of what this new
life change would mean for him. For a man who made his living
receiving money from people to cast curses and do readings, this
is no small change. Willem encouraged him to go home right
then and bring his voodoo paraphernalia to be burned on the
stage in front of everybody. He left right away, and some of the
people thought he would not return. About a half hour later,
he returned with a variety of items. Some of the men had built
a little fire on the stage. One by one, the new Christian tossed
his voodoo items in the fire and watched them burn. He paused
when he held out a rope. He nodded at Willem, who knew of
the special power this rope was said to have. When he tossed
the rope into the fire, it landed on the burning logs but didn't
burn. It just sat there in the fire for a long time. The evangelism
team looked on and prayed quietly. Finally, after what seemed
like five to ten minutes, the rope caught fire. As it burned, it let
out a scream that was heard by the entire crowd. The former voodoo priest knew the power of Jesus Christ that had changed his
life was greater than the powers that he had just burned in the
fire.

Roger was amazed with the life transformations that had
taken place that week. Roger exclaimed, "It was a phenomenal
week." The crowd grew every night because word spread about
the crusade. Each time, the service was a little different but the
emphasis was the same: God sent his son Jesus Christ who lived a
perfect life and died for our sins. Jesus is Lord!

Bill recalled some of the details, "Every day there had been
snafus and delays. The first night the soundman refused to come
up the mountain unless he got more money. Then his truck
broke down. Later, they had problems getting the system going.
Then the system went out completely right after the invitation to
the altar." It certainly seemed like there was more going on than

what they could see in front of them—a real spiritual battle waging behind the scenes.

Roger said, "The following Sunday, Willem held a church service in the new building and all seventy-seven of the individuals who gave their heart to Christ during he crusade actually showed up. Then for the next several months they became the church in Gramothe. The retention was amazing." The crusade was a week of intense work for each team member who came. They all had different supporting roles and together they worked to support Willem as the crusade made a difference the lives of the men and women of Gramothe.

On the evening of the team's last day, rain and dogs barking in a pecking-order altercation joined the drums to create an especially noisy night. The team was tired and looked forward to the final night's sleep, hoping that they would rest well in spite of the constant noise. The following morning, Willem and the team loaded up the truck with their suitcases and headed back to the airport. As they said good-bye, Willem faced them and one by one expressed his gratitude to each for his help and embraced each of the team members before they headed out of the country.

Since the first crusade, MTM has held other crusades in Gramothe; each one was powerful and had a great impact. MTM has also been involved with other crusades that were held in the area. In Haiti, when a church is having a crusade they typically invite all the other churches in the region who participate and forego their normal services in order to allow their people to participate. It's a huge event. There is an annual crusade held in Thomassin just a short drive away on a soccer field, and another crusade in Petionville, which is also very influential. MTM honors the tradition of helping her sister churches with these annual crusades.

Church Growth

The church in Gramothe officially began at the crusade. The following day, Willem assumed the role of pastor, teacher, general organizer, secretary, contractor, and anything else that was required. He started his teaching by repeating the essence of the message of Jesus Christ that Roger had delivered. Willem continued the preaching and in time began teaching the messages learned in the epistles about morality, and God's guidelines for living.

The church members grew in understanding of who God is and the world God made through Willem's preaching and through guest speakers who came with mission teams on a regular basis. Willem followed Haitian tradition and regularly invited any visiting pastor to the pulpit while Willem interpreted. Over the years, this has brought a rich blend of teaching to the church. Word spread throughout the village about the church because it was high quality and worth going to. The congregation slowly grew over the next few years as Willem continued to become involved in the lives of the people in the village. The church was not structured in a congregational (or democratic) style as is typical in North America. Rather a top-down structure was adopted where the leadership prays and makes decisions that affect the direction of the church. This style, while contrary to the American democratic mindset, fit quite well with the Haitian authoritarian structure.

Every Sunday morning they held a formal worship service. After the singing, individual small groups in the church conducted their weekly contest. In their small groups, they memorize scripture together as part of their Bible study, and each Sunday morning, they would recite their passage together in unison before the whole congregation. Several groups participate each week, and the winner receives a tapestry banner hung from a polished dowel to take back to their group. The winners were always very proud.

Willem dovetailed the scripture quiz into other activities that were happening in the village. Donors from the States wanted to help families in the village in various ways and gave money for a goat or a cow for one of the families. The Christmas season especially results in extra donations from various supporters. Some American families use money that they would have used for Christmas presents to give something big to a Haitian family instead. Willem always did his best to give the animals to families who and had been pillars in the church for a long time yet still had significant need.

One Sunday morning, Willem set up the scene in advance. He had selected a woman who had been with the church for some time to receive the donated goat. The scripture contest took place as it normally did each week and the banner was given out. Then Willem selected a number of individuals for a second contest. Acting like Howie Mandel before his crowd of cheering fans, he drew out the process in a bit of drama. After a series of questions, only one contestant was left, the woman Willem had planned to give the goat to. He set up the last question as the crux on which everything depended. Before delivering the question, Willem called out to a man at the door, "Bring it in!" A young man stepped outside then walked back into the church with a goat on a leash. A rustle of laughter rippled through the crowd. With the prize standing before them Willem raised up his arms with his palms down asking for silence; he could barely contain his own laughter as he turned to the contestant and asked the final question. He looked at her intently and waited for her answer. Enjoying the moment, she paused before answering. When she answered correctly a big roar of celebration filled in the church, as Willem handed the goat over to her.

In this village, a culture has been established that the leader portions out gifts from North Americans of all kinds on a regular basis. Willem provided the people with education through child sponsorship, and he also helped them out with food, clothing, medicine, and even building homes. Willem had always been careful to deliver gifts as fairly as possible as rewards for their dedication and involvement with the church, the school, or the efforts to help the village. In this setting it was obvious to the entire church was watching that Willem was giving away another blessing, but this time adding a huge element of fun to the process.

After the weekly scripture contest, Willem typically walked through some announcements and community issues. This could be anything from the progress on construction projects to hand-washing techniques. Seven years after the church began, a new bathroom facility was added. The new facility had six toilets and six sinks, and was kept impeccably clean. The bathroom promised to bring better hygiene to the village as a whole. It had been common before the bathroom was built to see men and women urinate outside next to the church before going inside. With large numbers of people relieving themselves in the same place, streams of urine flowed downhill from the church. With the advent of the new toilets, Willem wanted to open the facility to everyone who came, but this was a significant problem because much of the congregation had never seen a commode before and did not have the foggiest idea of how to use it. So Willem gave instruction on use of the toilets from the pulpit.

Willem had his deacons patrol around the church before and after the service. When people appeared as if they were about to relieve themselves outside the building, they were immediately directed to the bathroom. A number of individuals went inside the building, saw the clean white tile floors, shiny porcelain fixtures, and refused to soil the bathroom because it looked too clean to defile in such a manner. For several months, Willem announced from the pulpit about the proper use of the facility. In an effort to make his point as clear as possible, he would bend down in a semi squat position mimicking sitting on a toilet. Then, right there in front of the whole church, during his explanation of how to use the facilities, he would grimace and pretend to bear down as if having a bowel movement. The visiting Americans in the front row looked down at the floor and hid their faces in embarrassment, but the Haitians were practically taking notes! This instructional demonstration was necessary for those who had never seen the toilet, or who had gotten stage fright and had gone back outside to have a normal bowel movement the regular way—in the bushes. Week after week Willem gave instructions about the use of the facility, and the deacons enforced the new rules. Eventually their habits changed and everybody, young and old, was using the modern toilets on a regular basis.

The Dove

Every Sunday night, a less formal service was held and just about anything can happen on a Sunday night service. One visiting team came to the evening service, and Pastor Bruce Michael Lyle led worship. Michael recalled the evening. "There was a woman at the church who was tormented by demons. She went up for prayer while Willem was praying, and he called me up to pray for this woman. And so, we just started pleading the blood of Jesus over her, and it seemed like when we were praying, I just prayed for salvation.

"She was dealing with voodoo. And as she turned her heart to Christ, it was just miraculous. I'm praying, and Willem was watching and praying. A dove flew into the church and flew around the whole sanctuary of the church three times then stopped on the pillar. The dove just stayed there, it was unbelievable. When that dove flew around, the spirit that was within the woman disappeared, and there was total peace in the room. As we continued to pray after a while it just left. It was the most unique thing, I had ever seen in my life."

Now, doves just don't just hang out up there on the mountain.[2] Those who live there explain that they have never seen doves or pigeons in the region. Michael explained, "There is great significance of a dove as a symbol of the Holy Spirit and peace. God was saying, 'Hey, I'm here.' That was the coolest thing. You could really feel God's presence. I'll never forget it."

Every day of the week was a busy day for the church. The school met in the facility during the day, and each evening, there were activities for various groups. Each Tuesday, the women's group gets together. Sometimes it will be at the church, and other times it will be in a one of the women's homes; each week they gather to pray. Every Saturday night the men's group meets. They share, pray, and allow God to strengthen them through their fellowship. Each Saturday morning is the meeting of the youth group. With no school, they meet in the morning and do what youth groups normally do: play games, study lessons from the Bible, and challenge one another. On Wednesday night, the church meets once again for a midweek service. There are no good shows on television to pull members away from church. Neither are there any video games nor bowling leagues to keep people from coming. In fact most homes don't even have a light other than a candle or lantern at night. The best source of entertainment and activity

2　Five years after this incident, a couple of families began to raise pigeons about a half-mile from Gramothe. Since then, doves have been frequently seen flying through the valley.

in the village is right there at the church. So Wednesday night is reliably a busy service, with lots of people sharing and being involved.

Haitian's love music! A big part of the worship service is the music. When the church started, they had a few singers and an occasional conga drum. But it didn't take long for the visiting mission groups to bring along musical instruments that they donated to the budding church. When a keyboard arrived, musically inclined people flocked to the new apparatus. After a few short sessions, a talented young man began leading worship from the front of the church with this new instrument. After a few years, a drum set was donated. It sat in boxes, unassembled and unused for several months because nobody knew how to put the drum set together. A visiting pastor, who was also a drummer, noticed the drum set in the corner of the church on a Saturday afternoon. Immediately, he began putting the set together and tuning it. While he worked, a crowd of boys and young men anxiously awaited the demonstration of the new percussion miracle. He played in church the following morning along with the other musicians and within a couple of days, budding drummers were spending time mimicking what they had seen him do in front of the church. In no time, drummers were rotating on the drum set each week on the worship team.

Over the years, guitars have become commonplace, but they're not as prevalent as young boys and men who yearn to play them. A couple of men and women from the village have made a business of giving music lessons. The worship team can have as many as four electric guitarists playing together at a time. Passionate donors who want the best for Gramothe's church have donated the soundboard, microphones, amplifiers, cords, and speakers. Each Thursday night the music team gets together to worship together. They practice together for several hours, working on all sorts of musical progressions, and worshiping God together. Over the years, a number of talented people from the village have volunteered their time and energy on the worship team, giving of themselves as they honor the living God.

Four years after the first building was built, a lot of changes had taken place in Gramothe. The school had grown, with more classrooms and buildings beginning to creep up the hillside, and every child in the village was in the school. The village was a completely different place than it had been only a few years before. As people saw that Willem was doing more than just talking about a man named Jesus, but he was truly helping them, and they began to pay attention. With clean water, a medical clinic, and a thriving school, even the toughest critics would have to say, "Why is this guy doing all of this?" Men of all types approached Willem and asked him why he was there. This was the open door Willem had been waiting for. He explained that the love of Jesus was poured out in an amazing way on the cross, and what he was doing in the village was nothing more than an extension of Jesus' love for them. The village continued to improve as people put their faith in Jesus Christ. The five voodoo priests in the village had either become followers of Jesus Christ or had left the area. At night, it was rare to hear voodoo drums anymore. God had moved in a major way in the small church on the side of the mountain. But with the church growth came the problem of overcrowding and the need for more space.

In 2003, Willem made plans for a larger church building, which would enable them to accommodate their growth and continue to serve the village. With the help of construction teams that came down for that purpose and his skilled construction crew, he built a church that seats over 400 people and accommodates a large worship team and choir. Just outside the church he installed a white steeple with a cross on the top that is lit up each night like an airport. It is the symbol of Christ's victory over death and voodoo.

The Trek

I was visiting MTM and staying in Willem's home, and we were planning to go to church on a typical Sunday morning. When I met him at breakfast, Willem informed me that we would be going on a hike. He encouraged me to put on comfortable shoes, bring a change of clothes, and some water. This was a little unusual, since Willem normally ran the church in Gramothe. Church would typically start at about 9:30 or so and conclude some two hours later. But today we left early and got to Gramothe at about 8:00 A.M. Willem spent about half an hour hobnobbing with the folks at the church, and then he came over to where I was waiting with his nine-year-old son, David. Standing nearby was a group of nine well-dressed young men that I recognized as the young men's choir. Willem simply said, "Let's go." I looked at David and the choir, and we all headed toward an uphill path just to the left of the church.

As we walked past the small agricultural plot that abutted the MTM property, Willem said, "You see, I like to get things done. Some day, I would like to buy this property and build a nice entrance for the church." He pointed out where he would make a staircase and a foyer that would make for an elegant entrance for the church. "The owners aren't in the mood to sell right now, so we'll have to wait."

I had no idea of where we were going or how long it would take to get there. The rain-washed dirt path wound up the mountainside. Given the opportunity, it would test the limits of any four-wheel drive vehicle. As we climbed, we passed some fantastic vistas on the clear, windless 72-degree day. We enjoyed the beautiful white clouds, which striped the deep blue sky. We walked at a steady pace, and after a while my knees were aching and my legs were screaming for a rest, but there was no slowing of the pace.

Trying to keep my mind off my tired body, I asked Willem, "Do you have problems teaching the Bible to folks who can't read or write?"

Willem answered, "A lot of people in Haiti cannot read. Some people quote various numbers for the literacy rate, when I see those numbers I just laugh because there is no way for them to be even close. The fact is that many people cannot read, and so we deal with it."

I asked, "How do you set the requirements for membership or being a teacher or a deacon? Are they dependent on understanding and being able to explain God's word or on being able to read it?"

Willem said, "I tell you the truth, just because they can't read doesn't mean they are not smart. I didn't go to college like you did, but I have read the Bible with the Holy Spirit as my teacher. At first, we had reserved teaching and deacon positions for those who could read and write, in an effort to be protective of the

Word of God. But during a service one Sunday evening, I took a leap of faith and asked a man named Chantale Hyppolite to share from God's word. Mr. Hyppolite had been attending the Monday evening discipleship meetings for some time and had done very well, you know. He was a leader in the group even though he couldn't read or write at all. His understanding about the things of God was maturing from listening to the preaching of God's word and applying what he had learned. When he stood behind the pulpit, I tell you I was nervous at first. But as he opened his mouth to speak, I was surprised because the man spoke with the authority of the Holy Spirit. He gave a very encouraging message that night and that changed how we set teacher and deacon requirements within the church."

Willem explained that for those who want to go deeper and learn more about God, the opportunity is there for them, and they are encouraged to do so. The curriculum is the Bible and the lessons are straight from his word. Teaching includes every subject one could imagine: biblical doctrine, including the creation, Jesus' death and resurrection, and the trinity, as well as life application issues including worship, money, prayer, fasting, marriage, and family life. Those in attendance who can read keep a notebook chronicling the lessons, and those who can't read listen intently. Everybody is taught, and everybody learns.

We continued our uphill march and passed emaciated cows and horses, which were grazing on sparse weeds scattered on the hillside. Willem discussed how he took his family on trips to the United States each summer. These were essential for fundraising, reconnecting with churches in the states and organizational support of the ministry. Beth enjoyed the summer trips as the only time for her kids to spend time with her extended family. With the summer off from school, their kids enjoyed a vacation, and Willem and Beth enjoyed much needed time away from the rigors of missionary work. Back in Gramothe, the school was out for the summer, but the church needed to continue. Willem asked a number of men from the Monday night discipleship class to be pastors in training. They were in charge of keeping the church running during the summer. Not only would they preach but manage the worship team, the children's ministry, the youth group, the women's groups, and the weekly Bible studies. The first summer he left, Willem was biting his nails on a daily basis, concerned about the health and direction the church would take in his absence. After the first few years, he had trained a number of men who could do a good job keeping things going while he was gone. Some of these men have also been sent out from Gramothe to start churches in surrounding villages. The Gramothe church has had influence far beyond the geographical boundaries of the village.

As we came up to a scenic overlook, I asked where the other churches were who had been affected by the missionary work of the Gramothe church. Willem just grinned and said, "Oh, the villages on both sides of us have been changed for the better. You can't see them from here. We still have a little hike ahead, this church we are going to today sent down a choir a few months ago, so we are coming up there with our choir to visit them."

"Do they know you are coming?" I asked.

"Oh, no. We will talk to the pastor when we get there," Willem grinned.

I asked, "Who is preaching down in Gramothe today?"

"One of my deacons who is a very good guy," Willem responded.

"When did you ask him to preach?" I inquired.

Willem continued the steady march up the mountain and said, "Last night."

I laughed, "So you gave him twelve-hours notice that he would be preaching and running the service?"

"Actually less than twelve hours. People do their best when they have to rely on God, you know."

"Will he do a good job?"

"Oh, ya. He's a very good preacher and will deliver the word of God very well. I've heard him preach a number of times."

At about 9:30 we turned sharply up hill, took a small path up for another ten minutes or so, and then we came to a small flat region that held a thirty-by-seventy-foot cinder-block building with rebar sticking out all over the place. "We're here," Willem announced. It was a nondenominational Haitian Christian church.

I found a shady place behind the church to catch my breath; I took a sip of water, removed my dress shirt from my backpack, and switched it with the sweat soaked T-shirt that had served it's purpose. I noticed that Willem hadn't even broken a sweat. He explained that he runs in the hills early each morning to keep in shape to play on his soccer team. On the ground surrounding the building were pieces of plastic, paper, and Styrofoam rubbish strewn about and lining the base of the structure and the surrounding bushes. Just to the rear of the church, I noticed a few women huddled around a small fire and a couple of stainless steel cooking pots.

Willem made the rounds and greeted everybody there; it seemed like everyone knew him even though we were quite a distance from Gramothe. I saw that people gave me an inquisitive look when they noticed the pale-faced stranger in their midst, but then their eyes lit up when they saw Willem standing next to me. Men and women eagerly approached him and greeted him. In typical Haitian fashion, the pastor invited his guest to speak in the service, but Willem declined the honor and said that he would simply worship with them.

We headed inside and sat in the back of the church in the last row of benches. Rows of similar unpainted benches lined each side of the building, and they quickly become packed tightly with a mass of humanity. I heard a generator fire up outside, and the pastor began speaking through the microphone with a little feedback from the sound system. Suddenly, the worship service had begun. The band in the front of the church struck up an island style version of "Our God Reigns," and everybody sang it in Creole (except the solitary white guy in the back who was singing in English).

I felt underdressed in my jeans and running shoes because everybody else had on their Sunday best. The men wore dress shirts and ties along with slacks. The women wore nice dresses or what would have been called business suits in the 1980s. On their heads were coverings of various types. Some women had lovely lace coverings that they simply placed on top or tied around their heads. Some wore doilies; others had headbands of various colors and materials. A few women had washcloths simply placed on top of their heads and other women wore head pads that they use when they carry water buckets or other items on their heads. They just balanced the little pad on their heads as they sat in church. As the worship got going, they would rock back and forth and dance a little. The head coverings would fall off now and then just to be rescued by a nearby woman who would retrieve them and place them back on the head of the woman.

"Merci Senor, Hallelujah, *shita*," the pastor announced at the end of the first song. (*Shita* is the Creole word for sit.). In a brief moment of silence, I could hear the low hum of the generator again, but then the singing continued. After a couple of songs, the worship band went silent, and I heard drums beating outside. Slowly, a man carrying a base drum walked in the door. The blue bass drum was dented from years of use and had "Jesus pour Haiti" painted on the skin, it was rhythmically beaten by a confident man holding a branch with a tennis ball stuck on the end of it. A boy holding a snare drum followed him and another tapping a solitary cymbal on a string every few measures. A choir wearing matching turquoise robes followed the procession; they marched slowly to the front of the church as they continued singing.

About thirty minutes into the service some men behind us brought in another couple of ten-foot benches, and a few people sat on them. Ten minutes later they moved the benches a couple of feet forward and placed ten small chairs along the wall behind the benches. About five minutes later, a man wiped the benches off with a rag, and they were instantly congested with people. The building continued to fill and about an hour after the service had begun, and the back of the church was overflowing with well-dressed churchgoers. Over 300 men women and children packed the small place, giving no hope to abiding by any sense of a fire code.

The choir finished their songs and sat together in the front row; the pastor invited up another group. Nine women wearing matching green dresses and a variety of head coverings appeared through the crowd at the back of the church. They slowly danced their way forward, and after about five minutes, the train finally made it to the front. They assumed the position of a choir and sang another three songs, each a multiple of times. During all of this, each woman held a stick in her hand, which held identical banners that said Messagere Du Grand-Roi (Messengers of the Great King). They danced and waved the banners in synchronous movements as they sang.

The church was an industrial gray both inside and out; the concrete that had gone unpainted for many years. There were nine holes in the ceiling, each of which bore a trio of wires, red, green, and white. Some of these wires housed temporary light fixtures while others were bare. The light fixtures, which were in use, held a variety of types of bulbs, and only half of them were actually lit. The majority of the light in the building was coming in the four windows on each side, which also allowed a wonderful breeze since they were free of any glass, only covered with iron bars.

The choir finished their songs and was applauded enthusiastically. Next, a group of nine young men in white shirts and matching green ties then took their position at the front of the church. They wrestled with the feedback on the sound system for a few minutes before deciding to sing without it. They were talented and had beautiful voices and sang in harmonic acapella.

After this choir, the pastor made some announcements and another woman spoke for about ten minutes, acknowledging various people in the congregation. Then the music began once again, and they passed the offering plate. When it reached us, it had passed through the hands of over 100 people, yet less than 250 Gourdes (about $6 U.S.) in coins and bills were scattered in the bottom of the red plastic burger-serving basket. Willem put in a Haitian bill as he grasped basket and passed it to me. I passed it on, and when they had brought the collections back to the front, the pastor held them aloft like Kunta Kinte being recognized by the world. They gave thanks and invited another choir to sing.

By this time, I had lost interest in choirs. We sat through seven choirs over the course of two and a half hours before Willem elbowed me and asked if I needed to stretch my legs. I looked at David who had been perfectly behaved through the service and gave Willem an enthusiastic nod. We headed down the aisle to the exit. Once outside, we saw many of the previous choir members hanging out on the hard-packed dirt, along with the pastor. He spent some time with Willem and was proud to announce that the service would continue for another three and a half hours!

A couple of three-year-old kids intently stared at me. I chatted with them for a minute and gently shook their hands. They held my hand and rubbed my white skin. Willem said that I might be the first white person they had ever seen. Two more choirs came and went including the Gramothe men's choir, and we were taken to a small crowded building that housed the women who were previously laboring over the boiling pots and offered lunch. Willem explained to me that it was customary to serve lunch at church on special occasions. With a six-hour service I imagine that it would be mandatory to keep people in attendance!

Willem took two plates of beans and rice, and stepped outside. He gave the food to the members of the Gramothe choir, and he let them know that we were heading back to Gramothe. The morning's total choir count is unknown, and it's fair to say that about half of them entered the church by dancing slowly down the aisle.

When we had walked a few minutes with David bouncing down ahead of us, Willem commented on the experience. "This church will go on and on. People sing and dance for four, five, or six hours. That's too long. By the time the preacher gets up to speak, the people are falling asleep. How can they learn anything at that point?"

Willem told me about his efforts to help the local pastors. On Roger's second trip to visit MTM, Willem took him on a trip. They drove about two hours to a place where some American missionaries who were holding a pastor's conference. During the drive, Willem explained that the vast majority of pastors in Haiti are poorly trained and ill equipped to handle the needs of a congregation. They are loving men, with hearts of compassion, and generally good teachers and often they are good listeners; but most have a limited understanding of the scripture and little or no training in counseling. The result is struggling churches without the ability to train or equip men and women in godly living.

Roger and Willem arrived at a church in Port-au-Prince in mid-morning. They parked on the sidewalk and walked through the busy crowd to find a loosely organized array of men and women around the building. Inside were two white missionaries teaching a small group of black men. The pastors had come for bags of rice, which were promised to pastors who would sit through their teaching. This was a pastor's conference. Willem and Roger sat for about an hour listening to the teaching, it was good solid teaching about counseling and dealing with family conflicts. At the break, they greeted the missionaries then stood in the back. Willem looked over the bags of rice stacked along the wall and said to Roger, "This is what I want to do, but we should not bribe the pastors to come by offering them a bag of rice. These missionaries don't even know the harm they are doing by giving this rice away. It's rice harvest season right now, and this free food lowers the prices of the crops that the farmers have worked so hard to harvest. This is not the way to help."

Willem turned to Roger and said, "These pastors are good men and they need this conference, but they should come because the quality of the teaching is good, and they know the benefit they will receive will help their people." They headed for their car and together, Willem and Roger brainstormed about how to put on a better pastor's conference. They planned a conference in Gramothe with several guest speakers to talk on a series of topics. When the men had attended the courses over the curriculum of two years, they would receive a certificate of completion.

A few months later, once the arrangements had been made, Roger was a guest pastor at Willem's first pastor's conference. Twelve local pastors attended, and it was a valuable education time for everyone involved. They covered the basics of the gospel and how that influences daily life, emphasizing the value God places on their lives and how much God loves them. Later, in subsequent conferences, other venues were added. They held a series of afternoon sessions for the elders and deacons and covered practical day-to-day issues like basic pastoral meetings and how to deal with conflict. Then in the evenings they held meetings for the pastors and discussed biblical truths and included the gospel of Jesus Christ every time. Willem never gave them any rice or any gift other than the quality teaching they provided.

The pastor's conference continued and grew over the years. Every few months, guest preachers come and visit to pour into the lives of the local pastors. Always well attended, this conference has been a source of refreshing for hundreds of pastors who have come from near and far. As Willem explained the progress of the pastor's conferences, he once again referenced the marathon service we had just attended. "We've done a lot to help them, but we also need to focus on the length of the services,"

Willem said. "People like coming to weddings at our church because they last forty-five minutes or so. They don't drag on for three or four hours, which is customary. It's the same thing with funerals. They don't need to be long, and people even like coming to our funerals," Willem said with a chuckle.

As we walked down the steep path, he kept up a brisk pace for so long that my legs began to shake. We saw some Gramothe churchgoers coming up the mountain as we were heading down; the church in Gramothe had been dismissed for some time by then. Willem called out to each person by name, and they answered with a smile and a wave. Occasionally he would stop and chat with them, and my legs were grateful for the rest. Usually, however, he made a couple quick jokes and shared a few laughs as he continued downhill.

I changed the subject and asked, "Do you teach about tithing in your church?"

Willem said, "From day one, I taught them about the tithe. They don't get a paycheck every two weeks, but they get paid when they sell their crops at the harvest. That's when they bring their tithe in."

"Do they tithe in cash or in crops?" I asked.

"Oh, they bring in money only," he said.

"How does the church manage the money?" I asked.

"Every week the deacons count the money that comes in and they keep record of it. They use the money to run the church. They pay the music director who gets five thousand Gourdes a month ($125 U.S.), which is a fair salary in this area. They also pay for gas and other church expenses, but he's the only staff member that gets paid. The church buildings were built with money that was donated from people in the States, but it is sustained with money from the local people. I also encourage people to give beyond their tithe, and God blesses this. Ten percent is the baseline and beyond that is further offerings. They give their crops to a tuberculosis hospital, which helps a lot. I provide a truck for them to take their vegetables there, and they do the giving. This is an example of their offering."

I asked, "So most of the people in your church tithe?"

He answered, "Oh, ya. And our offering plates don't look as bare as that one you saw this morning. We'll have fifteen hundred to four thousand Gourdes ($37 to $100 U.S.) each week. People need to give in order to receive God's blessing, but the church itself also gives a tithe."

"What do you mean?"

"A long time ago a missionary friend of mine taught me that the church needs to give a tithe of the tithe. So we take a tenth of what comes in each month and give it to nearby churches. We tell the people in the church what we are doing, and I use this as a teaching tool to help the people understand the tithe. It builds their confidence in the church when they see us doing it. You talk to a lot of churches, and they are always hurting for money. It's because they don't tithe. God has blessed us because we do."

I inquired, "Do you tithe personally?"

"Oh ya."

After a pause, I pressed in, "Do you give to the church or do it in other ways?"

He answered, "I give to the church, but I also give in a lot of other ways. I'll be honest with you. I'm in position to see a lot of needs that people have. I can use my personal tithe money for a lot of needs. And I generally keep my giving secret. You don't want the right hand to know what the left hand is doing. I'll tell you one example. We have a lot of kids that go to high school outside of Gramothe, and we take care of that out of our own money. And we do other things as well."

As we made our way down the mountain, the choir members scattered taking various paths above the village on their way home. At one point, Willem stopped and was talking with some people, and he followed them to their home, where we sat and chatted for about fifteen minutes before heading back down the path that led to the church. The whole area had been all but deserted by then, the families eating lunch at their homes.

CHAPTER 8
LIVING WATER

Whoever is thirsty, let him come; and whoever wishes,
let him take the free gift of the water of life.

Revelation 22:17

The Petit Riveire de Nippes located far below Gramothe was the village's only source of water. Men, women, and children were all tasked with the daily water duty for the family using five-gallon buckets that they carried on their heads up the mountain. This arduous task was their only means of getting the essential water to their homes. The walk was long and steep, and their reward was merely dirty drinking water.

The entire community bathed in the same water used for drinking. Women and men stripped naked to wash in the river, and take their time to air dry before donning their clothes, filling their buckets, and heading back up the mountain. Mothers washed their family's laundry in the river. They labored over the clothes doing the best they could without soap to get them clean. Then they spread the clothes out on the rocks to dry while they remained there with the drying clothes so that nobody from a nearby village would run off with them. After adequate time for drying, they folded the clothes into bundles and carried them on top of their heads all the way back up the mountain to their homes.

The water that they shared with cows and goats had an untold number of parasites. As a result, most of the villagers, especially the children, had infestations of intestinal worms. Since they were unable to obtain an adequate diet, the limited food they did have had to be shared with the unwelcome guests. These kids were badly malnourished and underdeveloped. When the kids saw the doctor at the medical clinic in the village many of them (and quite a few of the adults) had worms. The treatment was medication to rid the body of the parasites, and more importantly they received education in hygiene, and with every dose of medication given out, they were instructed to boil their drinking water.

While it sounds like a very simple thing to do, the prospect of boiling drinking water in Haiti was quite involved. The actual time and difficulty it took to get the water in the first place was incredibly labor intensive. Boiling the water meant that they would have to obtain fuel to run a fire for several additional hours each day. Using kerosene or propane would be far too expensive, so the only logical choice was wood. However, wood was a scarce commodity and Haiti already had a serious problem of deforestation from previous years of poor resource management. Boiling their drinking water, therefore, was simply an insurmountable task.

When people heard the instructions for boiling their water they smiled at the doctor and received the medication. They nodded and agreed to boil their water. But when they returned to their homes, they inevitably went back to life as normal. A few months later, when they returned for another clinic visit, the next visiting doctor would tell them that that they were feeling sick because the worms had returned. Once again they smiled as they received the pills and hygiene instructions.

The river carried the water they needed, and this had been life, as they knew it, for generations. But the problem was in the water and to help, Willem had to find another source.

Finding a Way

How could they find another source of water? A well would be impossible to dig in this mountain but a stream above the village could be leveraged for use if there was one. Willem began discussing all these things with the village elders and they told him about a spring far away near the top of the mountain. It makes a small stream and has a little waterfall right at the source. They explained, "The spring is in a difficult place to get to, and there is no path. The spirits live in waterfalls so we will not go near that place."

Willem replied, "If it's a clean spring, that water can change your life, and the life of every single person in the village. Show me where it is. I'd like to see it."

That very afternoon, Willem and two village elders (who reluctantly agreed to show the way) took the treacherous hike up to the spring. They proceeded up the mountain starting at the school. From there they walked up the mountain through farm plots and trekked over and across a ridge with a stunning view of the valley below and the nearby villages. They traveled over a mile and a half when they finally saw the waterfall in the distance. Willem picked up the pace in excitement but noticed that his two companions had stopped at the end of the ridge. They refused to travel one step farther. Willem understood their fear and thanked his friends for being his guide and continued alone the rest of the way. He coursed down and across a valley then up into dense scrub brush all the way to a small waterfall that seemed to come right out of the face of the mountain. It created a small stream that turned north, traveling into a very steep inhospitable uninhabited valley before making its way into the main river below.

As Willem looked down the mountain he could see the village leaders in the distance and gave them a big wave. He spent some time at that site envisioning what it would involve to transform this spring into usable water for the village. This area was some 1,100 vertical feet above the school but within reach of the village if he could find the right technology. While he could not see the church or school buildings from where he stood, he knew the impact it would have if this fresh clean water could be delivered there. However, this was much more than a physical fight. It was a spiritual one as well. As he stood in the very place that the elders feared, he dreamed that this is the place that would bring them both physical and spiritual life.

On his next trip to the States, Willem shared his ideas with a number of people and got a variety of ideas. Some people said a pump would be required to get the water the distance that Willem required, and others simply shrugged at the project. Willem took his best advice and planned for a pump to run a one-inch line down to a cistern that they could build in the village. It would bring clean flowing water to the village for the first time ever.

The school was still in construction and a cafeteria was the next big construction project. Willem decided to put the cistern under the cafeteria where it would be safe, protected from outside contamination, and accessible when necessary. While the construction crew began digging, Willem began teaching. Everywhere he went, he explained that if they were able to pipe water into the village from up the mountain, it would change their lives. They would no longer have to carry their water up from the river every day. Their water would not be shared with the animals, and it would be clean and healthy. They would not have to bring the laundry down to the river, but they would clean their clothes in their homes. Most importantly, they would be healthier. After they were treated for worms, the worms would not come back, and their children would not be as malnourished. Willem taught this simple message along the roadside, in the church, at the school and made the message clear everywhere he went. After some time and preparation, the people began to see the idea as a real possibility and excitement grew. When they asked how the water could be brought down, Willem explained the labor involved the massive project, which included their involvement every step along the way.

Willem estimated that if the water source was reliable and continuous, it could be pumped down using black industrial strength flexible PVC pipe to bring the water to the cistern at the school. The black pipe was chosen for the project because of it has a remarkably simple design and was essentially indestructible. The large rolls of piping could be carried up the mountain using enough manpower and the right equipment.

Willem discussed this project while visiting friends and supporters in the States. Dave Smittson heard Willem talk about the water problem and was immediately interested. Dave was an elderly gentleman from Fort Wayne, Indiana and had never been to Haiti but caught Willem's vision. He believed God would do tremendous work through this project and donated $20,000 to the effort.

Construction

The cistern was built and two miles of piping was purchased with the donated money. When the first truck carrying the piping arrived, an excitement came over the village. As they unloaded the large coils of piping in the schoolyard, a crowd gathered. Men, women, and children offered to help. They all could see the benefit of clean water, and the entire village volunteered to help.

Willem climbed onto the back of the pickup truck, explained the details of the project, and then separated the workers into sections based on where they lived on the mountain. He gave each group a section of the piping and told them where and how to install it. He orchestrated how they would start at the water source and work their way down the mountain connecting each section of pipe as they went.

Many hands make light work. This very labor-intensive work required many hands. In the hot sun the hoards of people installed piping throughout the village in the prescribed locations. Each 200-foot roll of pipe weighed about ninety pounds and was difficult to carry. The task of hauling them up the mountain somehow fell on a group of boys six- to eight-years-old. Each roll was surrounded by a group of boys who lifted the large awkward contraption up into the air and lumbered up the mountain. None of the villagers were afraid to work and everyone pitched in to the project right away. After the piping had been completely installed and connected to the cistern, a small pump was installed at the source; the water was turned on and began to flow. It flowed all the way from the spring into the cistern that emptied through two additional black pipes at the bottom. These pipes went underground below the school courtyard to a public spigot. Two solid weeks of labor-intensive effort from countless men, women, and children made it happen.

When the water was turned on, and the people could see the fresh clean water freely flowing right near their houses, tears of joy came down their faces. Since most of the villagers lived relatively close to the school, the flowing water changed everything for them. One of the villagers, Madam Stephen, explained it this way, "Before the water, there was no hope in the village. There were times that we went to bed thirsty and slept with no water. After the water flowed, we saw progress."

Take it to the Next Level

After the initial water was brought to the village, a commercial plumber by the name of John Chorpenning visited Gramothe to see his old friend Willem. He had known Willem ever since the days at Hope Missions Outreach and had fallen in love with the Willem's vision. John was in his seventies but that did not deter him from climbing up the mountain all the way to the spring, where he spent some time surveying the project. Then, down at the spigot, he measured the water flow and noted that it took about four and a half minutes to fill a five-gallon bucket. The water was plentiful but slow.

John suggested a few changes. He planned to remove the pump and allow gravity to send the water down hill. He also wanted to add two additional water lines for the village using a considerably larger two-inch pipe that would substantially increase the water flow. John described a line that could go from the spring to a four-way distribution box, and then to the entire village. He envisioned spigots placed literally all over the village, so water would be delivered even closer to their homes.

When the pipe and plumbing supplies were delivered, once again, the village rallied to help. After the project was complete, there were twenty-seven spigots scattered throughout the village. The people were thrilled to have the water much closer to their homes. The flow was measured again and a five-gallon bucket was filled in less than forty-five seconds—six times faster than before! But the result they would see would be even greater than anyone had expected.

Every family in Gramothe farmed in one way or another; farming was the primary source of income for the village. There was no plot of land in the region that was not actively cultivated. A family's plot of land generally yielded one crop each year; it was planted at the beginning of the rainy season and harvested at the end of it. This crop was traded locally within the village for other essentials or if they had a big enough harvest, they could take it to the market and sell it for a modest profit. This had been their life for generations. They were doing their best to get by, but they had very little to eat and never enough spare money to provide other basic necessities.

When the new two-inch water line was completed, the crops had just been harvested from most of the fields, and the rainy season was not expected for another eight months. A few enterprising farmers saw the water as a new opportunity. Within a few days a couple of women and men were out in their fields planting crops again. This had never been done before. The neighbors began talking about the crazy people who were planting without rain! Every day, they would take a five-gallon bucket fill it at the nearby spigot and gently irrigate their fields giving each budding plant a little drink of water. In a creative burst of genius, they used the water from the spring to irrigate their fields.

During the next few months, most of the fields were dormant except a few brave farmers who had taken the risk and worked their fields every day. The crops flourished and yielded a bonus harvest that these proud farmers took to the market to sell. As soon as the harvest took place, the rest of the village plots teemed with workers who began planting although it was the middle of the dry season. They adapted to the new style of farming and immediately took advantage of the extended seasons they had. They planted as soon as they harvested and continued farming. Crop after crop they planted, rotating what was planted. Since there was a considerable difference in the price of the crops from season to season, they planted crops that were typically out of season. Then at harvest, they were able reap a harvest priced higher at the market. They planted crops that were typically out of season since they had the ability to grow crops predictably with their irrigation system. This new stream of income brought tremendous hope to the village. After a few seasons of tapping into this new opportunity, their hard work was paying off. Many families had a real income for the first time ever. Not only did they know where their next meal would be coming from they but were able to provide adequate clothing and other necessities for their families.

Even Better

As living water continued to pour through the water lines throughout the village other means of improvement were discovered. With Willem's blessing, some farmers used their hard-earned farming profits to purchase additional piping to extend the water even closer to their fields. If they irrigated their fields aggressively during the dry season, the water supply would be temporarily used up with little water reaching the cistern at the school. So at first, they developed a rationing system during this season.

During that time, Leroy Steury who had committed to volunteering in Haiti with MTM full time for six months took the long walk up to the waterfall with Willem; it was March, the end of the dry season, and with one look at the piping coming out of the mountain, Leroy immediately suggested using a dam so more would available. Willem, shocked by the simplicity of the idea said, "I can't believe I didn't think of that myself!"

Shortly thereafter, the construction crew was on the task. They made a number of trips up to the water source hauling tools, concrete, cinder blocks, sand, and rebar. They had plenty of experience with this sort of building but never in such a remote location. They built a dam and reinforced the black pipe, which emerged from the bottom of the structure. This simple engineering multiplied the amount of water available to the village for consumption and irrigation during the dry season.

In the clinic, the doctors knew about the water project would have on the general health of the people and were excited to see the impact it would have. Yet, they still saw many patients with worms and continued to prescribe the treatments as before. Over the course of a couple of years, however, they began to notice that people from Gramothe gradually became free from the parasites. They drank clean water and did not have to boil it. The living water had completely changed the village and lives had been changed forever.

The clean water gave Willem an illustration of God's love for his people. Once they saw this with their own eyes, they understood that Willem was a man who cared for their well-being and was there to help them in any way possible. It was then that their ears became much more attentive to hearing his message of God's love through Jesus Christ. Standing next to one of the spigots, Willem took a cup and filled it with clean, life-giving water, and explained to every village resident the story of the woman at the well from the fourth chapter of John. In this story, Jesus simply asked a woman for a drink of water and this started a great teaching on who God is. In the conversation Jesus says, "The water I give will become a spring of water welling up to eternal life" (John 4:10). Water brings life, and Jesus brings eternal life.

When asked to remember the water from old times, the villagers remembered hauling it, and that their kids hauled it as well. They also remembered the diseases and death it brought. Willem explained that this is what Satan brings: disease, extra work, and the end result is death. God, on the other hand, provides pristine water that flows right to their homes. God provides life through his Son Jesus that is clean it is given freely and brings life. He held up the cup and looking over the group of people he had grown to know and love, he declared that the Jesus is the living water spiritually, just like the water in the cup is living water physically.

Catastrophe

In the spring of 2009, five years after the water was originally brought to the village the newness of the water had faded. No longer did they talk about how great it was to have the water nearby, but the flowing water was simply their way of life. It was then that catastrophe struck.

A disgruntled man who had a grievance with someone in Gramothe took out his frustration by attacking the water line. Very close to the water source, he wreaked havoc on the line with a machete and managed to dismantle it. This in itself is no small feat because the tubing is incredibly strong. With the line in pieces, the water immediately stopped flowing, and the village dried up because of his devious vandalism. The fields no longer were irrigated and the school's water supply stopped.

The people were outraged and formed a mob intending to kill the perpetrator. Since they had installed the pipe with their own hands, it was theirs to protect, and they wanted justice. Willem intervened and immediately brought in the Haitian legal authorities who began an investigation to find out who was responsible. During this process, the Haitian justice department determined that the charge to be placed on the criminal would be crimes against humanity. This is the same charge that was brought against Saddam Hussein for the slaughter of 300,000 of his people.

In a unique Haitian quirk, the police were very clear that the water line should not be repaired until justice was rendered. This forced the village to go on without water until justice could be served while they sorted out the legal side and investigated the crime. Until then, the line remained unrepaired, and the water did not flow. Life went back to how it had previously been for Gramothe. Long treks down to the river every day for water once again became a necessity. Imagine the look on a eight-year-old girl's face when she was handed a five-gallon bucket and told to go a mile down the mountain for water!

"Are you kidding?" She'd say. "Why don't we go to the spigot?"

"Because it's broken. Now go to the river," her mother would reply.

"I can't carry water all that way! It's too far!"

"I did it all my life before we had the living water. Now it's your turn. Pick up the bucket."

An entire generation of kids who have never carried the water for the family had to experience the daily labor of carrying water. To the relief of many children and parents alike, the line was repaired in the fall. The entire village held a party once again to celebrate the restoration of their living water.

Springs are relatively common in the mountains of Haiti. Villages like Gramothe throughout the countryside are equipped with the natural resources that made this water project possible. This entire project could be replicated in other villages for the benefit of the people all across the country. The process is complex and the labor involved in the effort is daunting, but this living water was brought about by the villagers' own sweat and is owned by those same individuals. Willem has looked into opportunities to embark on water projects and soon this may come to pass as a significant blessing to another Haitian village as a step in the effort to defeat generational poverty.

Willem took a series of pictures of the spring during the rainy season that showed the water overflowing the top of the dam and the black piping extending down the mountain. These framed pictures are now prominently displayed in the front of the church so that the people would remember the source of the living water that they continue to enjoy.

CHAPTER 9
GET ME A DOCTOR

Jesus said, "It is not the healthy who need a doctor, but the sick."

Matthew 9:12

When Willem brought in the mission team for MTM's very first evangelistic crusade, Pastor Roger recruited a nurse named Bill Rolfson to come with them as the medical arm of this mission. Bill responded, "Well, no, I don't mind. I mean that's what I do and that's what I'm trained for. But an arm? A little toe, maybe." Roger explained that the plan was for a Haitian doctor to run the clinic, and Bill to work there along side him as a nurse.

Bill worked in the Intensive Care Unit at Hendricks Community Hospital in Indiana. With his five years of experience, he was accustomed to putting together complex medications on continuous infusion pumps to care for heart attack victims or patients with severe trauma and lots of medical needs. He explained, "A doctor can tell me what the underlying problem is, and I can begin to anticipate the treatment protocols he'll order: antibiotics, cardiac medications, gastrointestinal medications, skin care, and patient teaching. That's my world in the ICU. However, I'm not trained in making those orders, and I'm not used to fixing cuts, scabies, or dealing with pregnancies." As far as medical care was concerned, this was definitely out of his comfort zone.

"When we got to Haiti on a Saturday. Beth and Willem were calling me 'Dr. Bill.' Well, call me what you want, but I told them that I would be just fine being a nurse, assisting the doctor. They both looked at me for a very long second then Willem laughed, 'There's no Doctor! You're the doctor!' I was sure they were joking. And they were equally sure I was kidding, but as I stood there listening to them explain that a doctor 'might' be there Thursday, I became utterly horrified! I'm not sure but it had to show on my facial expression. And when they told me with a straight face that I might deliver a baby, I almost regretted coming. My comfort zone was dissolving faster than an Alka-Seltzer."

Bill's First Clinic

Bill had not brought much in the way of medical equipment, but he did have first aid supplies and a suitcase full of medications. Each evening they sat at Willem and Beth's dinner table and divided the larger bottles of aspirin, Tylenol, and multivitamins into smaller units to easily dispense the following day.

With Willem's help, they set up a tent using a couple of sheets held up with some sticks and rope. They brought in a table and a couple of five-gallon buckets, which served as chairs. After Willem spread the word that the tent was for medical care, a crowd soon formed. Bill sat down inside the tent with his interpreter, Matthew, and went to work. He his first patient was a little girl who was there with her mother. He asked them what their medical problems were and examined them as much as he could without disrobing too much; there was no area for real privacy. Bill saw all kinds of ailments. He recorded in his journal:

The first little girl we saw had these infected little sores on her legs and bottom. She was such a cute little stinker, a little tomboy; which by the way, most Haitian people are small. I believe it has something to do with nutritional deficit. But back to the girl, I showed her mother how to keep the sores clean and how to apply Bacitracin, which I gave her.

Admittedly there were a lot of little ailments. For instance, this girl complained of stomachache with no other symptoms. Her pain didn't occur all the time, and it "went away" after she ate. So we told her to snack a little more often. There were a few situations where I felt completely helpless like with some like some ear and eye infections, skin problems, or throat infections; all I could tell them is the most basic: clean, irrigate, and gargle.

Everyone that I saw got a little packet of vitamins that they were instructed to break in half and take the half each morning with breakfast,; I advised them to drink plenty of water and bathe each evening This also applied for prenatal care. Beth, who was three months pregnant, pointed me in the right direction. She kept reminding me to think in the most basic, simplest terms, and when I got there, get even more simplified.

Most of the adult complaints centered around abdominal pain (only a few actually called it gas) as well as back and/or leg pain. The back and leg pain is pretty ubiquitous. Well duh, they carry five-gallon buckets of water halfway up a mountain on top of their heads then sleep on a thin pallet at night. It's a wonder they even have any discs left in their back after all that. This one girl age thirty-two couldn't even carry anything on her head and that was her main complaint.

This one elderly lady came complaining of a racing heart rate with activity and pain in her legs. Okay, now I felt useful! I'm back in my element of adult internal medicine. She walked away with vitamins and some aspirin with instructions to take half an aspirin with food and decrease her sodium intake. I only wish I could have done more for her.

This eighteen-year-old girl came up and complained of sore breasts. Beth had her lift her shirt, and I was shocked (though maybe not as much as Mathew). She had draining scabs covering her entire areola bilaterally. She said she had been to the clinic, and they had told her there was nothing that could be done. I can only imagine what damage that could cause to her self image. We gave her hygiene instructions and Bacitracin. Knowing that we had one more thing to offer her, I asked Mathew how to say, "Jesus is Lord." He said, "Jesu se sever." I used that line a lot the rest of the week.

There was this one woman who I was worried would just die right there, she was so, so, sick, and I didn't know what was wrong except that her heart rate was 120 beats per minute. She hurt all over, and she could hardly sit up.

Several families in a row presented with abdominal problems that were consistent with worms. I told Beth about it, and she brought the families together right there and taught a session on prevention of intestinal worm infestation.

One of the patients we saw was a skinny little girl who wore a yellow shirt and short pigtails. Her father brought her in and was concerned about her right eye. Her eye was so swollen that it was almost shut, and the infection was just dripping out. I kept thinking I would ask the doctor when he arrived regarding ophthalmology ointment. Beth reminded me to keep it simple. Okay, no ointment. So I taught the dad the following instructions:

1) Wash your hands.
2) Clean as much as possible with this saline wipe.
3) Throw the saline wipe away.
4) Cover it with this gauze and sleep on her right side to keep the left eye clean.
5) Keep fingers out of the eye.
6) Take a half a children's Tylenol twice a day.
7) Do this twice a day.

They told me the doctor would be there Thursday, so I kept thinking about that girl's eye for the next two days.

After clinic the whole team walked a little ways up the mountain into the "town." This was major *National Geographic* material. We saw many of the people who visited the clinic. We came across this other woman sitting outside her hut weaving reeds for a basket. After a little dialogue, she stated that she had a daughter who was crazy and had to remain tied up. Roger asked if we could pray for her, so she took us to see her. She was literally tied to a wall post of the shack. It was a pitiful site. She was a beautiful girl about twenty-years-old. She kept alternating between whispering and laughing; then just as quickly she would get this look of fright in her eyes which broke my heart and angered me at the same time. There wasn't anything medically we could do for her. We all prayed for her. Finally after we were done, I held her hand and said good-bye.

Debriefing

Bill experienced more new situations in one day than he normally would in any given year. Matthew quickly learned the routine and was very helpful. At the end of the day, they walked back to Willem and Beth's house and collapsed on the couch. Bill swapped stories with the rest of the team.

Pastor Roger said, "Hey, Dr. Bill how many patients did you see today?"

Bill was quick to respond, "Don't call me 'doctor!'" He was insistent that he was practicing nursing and did not want to be confused with a doctor. While he learned about the crusade, the rest of the team learned about many of the patients he had seen. Bill expressed how helpless he had felt and that many times, all he could provide was simple hygiene instructions and Tylenol.

During the course of the conversation, Willem explained that these hygiene instructions were absolutely new to the villagers. Nobody had ever told them to wash their hands before eating, boil their water, or bath their children daily. With these simple instructions, repeated over and over, Bill had made a huge difference in the lives of many people on that first day of the clinic. With this information coming from an American (the dominant culture), they immediately believed what he said, and the impact was tremendous for the Haitian people.

They had a delicious dinner of chicken Creole, white rice with bean sauce, split string beans, and beet salad (mixed with mayo and potatoes just like a potato salad). Then they prepared to do it all again the following day.

Ears

Clinic continued in the same vein for the next couple of days. Challenging situations continued with each new patient, and Bill did his best with each and every one. On Wednesday, a ten-year-old girl arrived at the tent accompanied by her mother and complaining of pain in her right ear. Her earlobe was red and had swollen to several times its normal size. A small piece of wood was stuck right through the earlobe. The other ear also had a little stick through the lobe but wasn't swollen or sore. This little girl had pierced her ears using a stick and now had an infection that was becoming serious.

The treatment for this is to remove the source of infection and provide antibiotics. Even without antibiotics available removing the foreign body was absolutely required for this girl. So Bill, Beth, and Matthew worked together and told the girl and her mother that they had to remove the stick so that her ear would heal. They were very resistant and did not want the stick removed, since that would ruin their work of having her ears pierced. When Beth told them that this was a serious infection and the child would lose her ear if she weren't treated, the girl and her mother finally relented and the mother quickly reached up and pulled out the stick with her fingers and a stream of pus poured out of the earlobe! They also removed the stick from the other ear, and gave her hygiene instructions and a warning to never pierce their ears in this way again.

Other girls came with similar infections of the earlobe, and some had tied string in a little loop through their earlobes to hold the holes open. Some of the strings had become infected and pus ran from the earlobe down the length of the string and dripped onto their shoulders. Bill and Beth removed the strings and counseled them on proper hygiene. Each time, the hardest part was convincing the people that the source of infection had to be removed.

Get Me a Doctor!

When Thursday finally arrived, to Bill's delight a doctor actually did came up to the village. The doctor was originally from Africa but now lived and practiced in Haiti. Bill was thrilled. He wrote in his journal:

> The doctor and I both worked side by side, we each had a chair for patients and a prescription pad. After we gathered

data we would send them out to the "waiting room" while Beth would fill the scripts, dispense, and teach. We saw forty-two patients in about four hours; the clinic was a great success that day. The doctor was able to diagnose just from looking at them. Scabies, ringworm, and head fungus were all easily treated with meds I didn't have but will return with next time I come.

I think the brightest part of my day was when this guy came with his daughter, a skinny little girl with a yellow shirt and short pigtails. After a minute of two of looking at her, I finally recognized her as the same girl who had the severe eye infection just two days before. But now I barely recognized her! The weeping was no more and the swelling was nearly completely gone. Bene Swa Latinele!

I'll be back later this year with plenty of supplies. I'm making a list and checking it twice. It's just wonderful having a doctor to offset a nurse. He's more "cure" oriented and a nurse is more prevention oriented. I can't wait till I get back.

Haiti's Medical Condition

Haiti struggles in many areas, and the poverty stricken country as a whole has very limited medical care. There are not enough doctors or nurses for the population, and their ability to treat the thousands of sick and hurting is severely limited in many ways. Even though Haiti is equipped with it's own universities and a medical school, she has continually lacked adequate numbers of medical personnel.

Anthropologist Timothy T. Schwarz spent several years in Haiti studying the effectiveness of humanitarian aid programs. In the process also had numerous experiences with the medical system in Haiti. After further investigation he reported his findings:

The Haitian medical system is a failure. Here's how the system works: The Haitian state has a medical school and, in exchange for providing free education, the state requires public service from all graduates. The students are supposed to spend two years working in clinics located in remote provincial areas or urban slums. But each year about half the new Haitian medical graduates legally emigrate directly to the U.S., without repaying the State for their education or doing a year of resident community service. The others take their residencies at clinics throughout the country, typically spending no more than a few weeks in the field. During their short stay, those who have any sense of commitment are able to confirm what they too already knew, there are insufficient medicines, bandages, and clinic aides for them to perform their job. In despair, most subsequently make the problem worse by taking whatever equipment and medicine there is and carrying it back to Port-au-Prince or some other urban area to set up in their own private clinic. Most also stay all their lives on the government dole as doctors on the rosters of a public hospital where they show up for work long enough and often enough to take any new medicines and equipment and lure away those patients who can pay. They spend the rest of their time in their private clinics, sometimes right down the street from the public hospitals were they are supposed to work, and from which they collect their small monthly checks.

Meanwhile, people of the rural areas and the slums continue to die in appalling numbers from curable diseases that are all but completely absent in developed countries.

Schwartz also shed light on the nature of the Haitian medical school in recalling a discussion with his doctor friend:

"I remember on orientation day at medical school in Port-au-Prince," he goes on. "The professor who was giving us the orientation speech said, 'You are here for money and you better have your own money. You need a car, you need money for books, for your office and for your clothes. And when you take care of a patient the first thing you ask is for his address. Not because you want to check on him. Non. Because he is going to owe you money and you will need to know where he lives so that you can collect it.' That's what he said. Not that we should care about patients and be honest or that we are helping. Non. He said that medicine was a business and it was all about money."

Before the 2010 earthquake, it was estimated that there were thirty hospitals in Haiti serviced by a total of 400 physicians. Half the doctors are in Port-au-Prince and a fourth are in other principal towns, leaving a minimum of medical services for the rural population. Although many statistics in Haiti are unreliable and Willem laughs whenever people quote numbers because they usually have little basis in research or real facts, a few numbers will help illustrate the demographic picture. It has been reported that in Haiti there is one doctor for every 7,180 inhabitants and one nurse per 2,290 persons. This works out to a ratio of 0.2 doctors and 0.4 nurses per 1,000 people. In comparison, in 2000 the United States had a ratio of 2.9 doctors and 9.4 nurses per 1,000 people (fourteen times as many doctors and twenty-three times as many nurses). In 2001 Haiti's infant mortality rate was rated at 95 per 1,000 live births, compared to seven in the United States. The life expectancy was sixty-one, compared to the States, where it is seventy-eight.

Many tropical diseases have been left untreated and have to spread to epidemic proportions. Malaria and Dengue fever thrive in the mosquito-infested villages where no treatment is available. Tuberculosis spreads easily through closely contained huts that large families are packed into. In the early 1980s, there was a prevalence of sexual tourism in the cities. This caused a rapid and epidemic spread of HIV/AIDS, which is now estimated to affect approximately 7 percent of the entire population but up to 80 percent of the Port-au-Prince prostitutes. In addition to these infectious processes, other common diseases such as coronary artery disease, diabetes, and asthma affect the population just as much as in any developed country but remain largely untreated.

Not only are there not enough medical providers, medical care is simply not affordable for the vast majority of the population that lives in abject poverty. With a limited household income or unemployment, the basic necessities of life are simply left out. With such poverty, many families cannot afford to feed their children adequately, much less provide them with clothing or an education. Paying for medical care when they get sick is simply out of the question.

What can be done about such an overwhelming problem? When faced with this question, Willem simply smiled and said,

"Make a difference for each one, one at a time." While sweeping reform and years of education for the population as a whole is necessary to change the country, right there in Gramothe, one small clinic is making a difference.

Dr. Marcia

Marcia Favali was a family practice physician in Terre Haute, Indiana, who was planning on going on an African safari with her twelve-year-old son, Andrew. However, the trip was cancelled because the travel agency was unable to recruit the required number of people to go. Just as she got word of the trip's cancellation, Pastor Brian McBride of Cross Tabernacle Church in Terre Haute asked if she would go to Haiti with him. Marcia said, "Well, sure. I've got my passport, and I've got time off. I'll go with you."

Marcia had never been overseas. She occasionally volunteered her services by providing medical care to indigent patients through a local program for patients without insurance. But other than that, she had no experience in missionary medicine at all.

Brian's team consisted of four women and nine guys, including Andrew. After Bill returned home, he had shared his experience in Haiti with Pastor Brian, a mission's pastor who was quick to prepare another team of people from a variety of local churches. There were two doctors, Dr. Marcia and Dr. Ken Sproul, and they obtained a supply list based on Bill's recommendations. They had antibiotics, antacids, antifungal creams, bandages, and everything that they thought they would need.

Marcia prepared for the trip by brushing up on her Spanish. She recalled, "The name of the island was Hispaniola, so I figured they must speak Spanish. I was all ready from my five years of high school Spanish, and I even had my little dictionary with me. When I got there and hear people saying "Bon Jour" and "Oui," I was like, 'What? No, Hola! Hola! Wait, what's going on?' My Spanish didn't work out very well."

The team set up clinic in the new building that was being built at the school for the kindergarteners. The concrete had just set but there were no windows or doors. This would have to wait for a week because the medical clinic was to be held right there. The room was very hot, there was poor lighting, and almost no ventilation. The team made no complaints but diligently set up two stations for patient treatment and a separate area for the pharmacy.

Angie McBride who was a medical receptionist back in the States, served as the pharmacist. The pharmacy consisted of suitcases that they had loaded up with medications, and Angie sat nearby packaging and delivering the medicine at the doctors' request. Each morning, they brought the suitcases up and every evening they took them back to Willem's home, since there was no way to lock everything up at night.

There was a small bench in the little room and everything was out in open, nothing was private. The work in the clinic went much like Bill had done with limited examinations and treating scabies, worms, and everything they could. When they needed a break for lunch, they had everyone leave the building and ate in the same little room where they held the clinic.

In the clinic, they saw hundreds of people. Word had spread about the clinic, and people came not just from Gramothe but from the surrounding areas. Many people walked for days for the chance to see the American doctors. The line grew, and people became unruly. Willem used his system of managing the line using tickets for each patient instituting rules for their conduct both while waiting in line and in the clinic. Many people came with voodoo paraphernalia tied around their waist or shoulders. Willem made it clear that Jesus was Lord there, and the clinic was not promoting voodoo and would not tolerate voodoo. If the people relied on their voodoo spirits, then they could not ask for help there. Willem made it clear that the clinic was simply an extension of Jesus' love and those who asked for treatment were receiving the love of Christ and their voodoo had no place there.

On Wednesday, it rained heavily in the afternoon. The hundreds of people waiting in line scrambled for cover and a scuffle broke out. Willem saw the fighting among the patients and immediately closed the clinic for the day. "This is not how you are to behave." He said, "If you want to see the doctor, you will have to come back tomorrow, and you will have to wait quietly and respect one another. Today we are done."

During the week, they saw hundreds of patients and ran out of most of the medications they had brought. The team attended church on Sunday morning, and on Monday they were ready to head out. Marcia recalled, "When I got on the plane heading to Miami, I thought 'I'm never going back there.' I mean, I like Willem and Beth, but the whole thing was just crazy. The whole process of lugging those old suitcases up and down that old road. My goodness! A week there was just too much."

A couple of months later, in 2001, Pastor Jim Evans planned the second trip around Marcia being there. The team had been assembled and they had nurses and a complete team, except Marcia. That's when Pastor Jim asked her to come. Very reluctantly, Marcia agreed to go again. "I really don't know why I agreed to come back that second time. But I'm very glad that I did. I've really enjoyed going there, and the clinics have been a tremendous help for the people, I'm just happy to be a part of it."

Dr. Marcia has returned to MTM on numerous occasions along with other U.S. and Canadian teams. After the first twenty trips, she lost track of how many times she's visited Haiti to see patients in the Gramothe medical clinic. Her daughter, Caitlyn, started helping in the clinic when she was nine-years-old. For the team members, running the clinic was just a part of the overall process. The trips were opportunities to serve Christ and to learn from the Haitians as they served.

During one trip it rained the whole time Marcia's team was there. They normally rode the truck up to the clinic each day, but one day that wasn't possible. She recalled:

"After clinic, it got dark and was raining really hard. Willem told us that it was too dangerous for the truck to go down the mountain, so we had to walk back. I was slipping and sliding all over the place walking down the road. The interpreter was on one side of me trying to hold me up, I was covered in mud, and when I looked at him, I saw that his shoes weren't even dirty. He had skill in walking up and down slippery mountainous terrain that I didn't have. After helping me and supporting me for a long time, he just looked at me and said, 'Listen, you walk where I walk and step where I step.' So I walked behind him and did what he did and everything was fine. But then we came to a series of great big rocks, and he just walked right down the center of them. I thought, 'I'm going to slide.' And right on the side was this grassy area where I could walk around those big rocks. So I walked up on the grass instead of walking where he walked, and I start sliding all over the place, and he didn't come to help me, he just stood there with his arms crossed. So I very meekly got right behind him and walked where he walked and stepped where he stepped, and we got down. It was the perfect illustration to following Christ."

Dr. Gingerich

As MTM was developing it's church and school. Teams continued to come on a regular basis. Willem encouraged all types of people to come and visit. One of the first was Dr. Gingerich. A family practice physician, Dr. Gingerich jumped at the opportunity to serve in the clinic and helped Willem design and build a permanent clinic, so that medical teams could see patients in an environment designed for patient care and not disrupt the classrooms. The clinic had four patient treatment areas, an administrative office, a pharmacy, and a storage room with plans for electricity in the future. When the clinic was completed, the medical teams enjoyed the comfort of private patient treatment rooms, which were separated by curtains, so they could have patients disrobe and perform complete physical examinations in privacy. Each patient had his blood pressure and other vital signs taken; patients were able to have other auxiliary tests such as pregnancy screening, fetal Doppler, and even minor surgical procedures. The pharmacy was stocked with a broad array of medications, and the teams were able to leave their medications and supplies each night after the clinic was closed and locked up.

When a physician came for the first time, they would be challenged with disease processes not seen very often in the States. Since the pharmacy is limited, and lab studies were almost negligible, different doctors would address the same diseases in vastly different ways. This resulted in confusion among the villagers. A person would be seen at the clinic three times for the same problem and be treated three completely different ways. If it could be standardized and streamlined, patient care would be better.

After several trips, Dr. Gingerich began formulating treatment protocols for the numerous tropical ailments that were treated in the clinic. Each diagnosis was equipped with a standardized treatment protocol that when used by each visiting physician over the years, provided a stable and affordable treatment for the population of patients at the clinic.

In many third world clinics around the world, medical providers will make their treatment protocols based on what the doctors see as being the best care, but they don't always ask the patients. Medical doctors will sometimes refuse to treat lice, scabies, or even intestinal worms since these ailments have a proclivity to return in a short period of time, especially if the underlying hygiene is not completely overhauled. The thought is that if they are only able to treat a child for lice for a couple of weeks, and it returns, then the treatment was done in vain.

However, when viewed from the patient's perspective a different conclusion is drawn. One gentleman who was raised in such a poverty situation and is now a part of mission teams to help the poor explained it this way, "If I had two weeks free of lice when I was a kid, it would have been the best two weeks of my life!"

Treating people with problems that have a tendency to return is not the most rewarding treatment for the medical provider, but it certainly can be appreciated by the patient just as much as any other type of major medical treatment. As Sharon Johnson said, "Jesus is all-inclusive, and even the small ailments deserve treatment." The patients should help determine which treatment modalities are appropriate to pursue, and which are not necessary. Willem has done this. When Dr. Gingerich developed the protocols for treatment, he worked through the eyes of a native son of Haiti to see what the patients truly want and need. In doing so, the treatment protocols have been tailored for this population of people. Dr. Gingerich honed his list over the course of several trips and included most of the ailments that would be seen in any given clinic. He printed them off and made them available for all the doctors and nurses at each treatment station. Visiting doctors many years later study the laminated sheets on the first day of clinic, and still find Dr. Gingerich's work to be extremely helpful in streamlining care.

Quality Assurance

As the clinic has grown and matured, requirements have been made for who can treat patients. Through Willem's experience growing up in Haiti, he knew that missionary organizations sometimes allow medical care to be delivered on the mission field in a way that would never be allowed in the United States, where licensure is very strictly guarded, and hospital privileges are only given to those with the proper credentials. However, on the mission field, nurses or even well-meaning college students can be found performing surgical procedures. The patients are smart, and they can tell whether the person standing over them holding a scalpel is an experienced surgeon or someone with no experience and has never performed a surgery before. These patients stay in the village year after year, while the visiting missionary goes home. Willem not only has to deal with the patients who stay in the village, but he is committed to representing Jesus Christ for them and delivering medical care as the hand of Christ.

The medical treatment that MTM provides through volunteer medical professionals should be the same high standard that they provide to their own patients in the States. In order to maintain this high standard of care, when a medical team comes, only licensed physicians are asked to provide medical care; licensed nurses are asked to provide nursing care. Only licensed dentists provide dental care. The goal in having providers only provide the type of care in Haiti that they provide back home is that each provider will be able to give their best.

Each patient who is seen pays a small fee—about three cents. This small co-payment is commonly done in American indigent care clinics. This is necessary to have so that the patients take some ownership of their care. Once they are registered as a patient, they wait in line for anywhere from a few hours to a few days and receive the care that can be provided by the team present. Sometimes, when teams bring numerous doctors, and the clinic flows efficiently, every patient who comes can be seen. Often, however, the vast numbers of patients can be overwhelming, and many simply can't be treated in the amount of time the team has; a line of patients must be turned away and given tickets that will reserve their spot in the line the next day.

Sonia

A nurse named Anna came with a team from Iowa to work in the clinic. The team of eighteen included three doctors, four nurses, and eleven nonmedical personnel who came to serve as needed. One of those was Karen who worked as a secretary. She had no medical training, but she offered to help out in any way possible. The team was treating patients with all the typical clinical problems. Soon, both Anna and Karen both felt comfortable in the new environment with diverse challenges and dove into their work.

A beautiful nineteen-year-old girl named Sonia Louis came to the clinic with a huge infected cyst. The mass, about the size of a baseball, protruded above her clavicles and extended to her larynx. Through our interpreter, they learned the lesion appeared several years earlier. A Haitian doctor had performed surgery to remove it, but it returned a few months later. She then sought the care of the voodoo witch doctor who treated it with traditional methods. It worsened. Ostracized by her village, Sonia struggled to survive.

As Anna assessed Sonia's condition, pus dripped from the infected cyst, producing a putrid odor. With no access to bandages, Sonia had covered the cyst with a small leaf to absorb the chronic drainage. But she couldn't cover—or escape from—the smell. Anna asked the surgeon Dr. Shanu Kothari to examined Sonia. After a quick assessment, he knew he must excise the cyst immediately. Karen and Anna set her up for surgery. Sonia lay comfortably on her back while we prepped and draped her neck. Dr. Kothari injected Lidocaine around the area. He held the scalpel, paused a moment, then stepped back to the back counter and put on a mask with a full visor attached and continued. As he made the horizontal incision, a stream of yellow fluid shot up covering his entire mask and eye shield.

A powerful stench filled the clinic. Karen, unaccustomed to such surgical situations, dashed across the room yelling, "Oh, the smell, the smell!" Since the windows were open and a slight breeze was going through the clinic, she actually ran downwind from the patient, right into the thick of the putrid odor. With no way out, she had to endure it. The rest of the team, whose noses had been dulled from years of medical treatment, enjoyed an unexpected chuckle.

Dr. Kothari replaced his mask and eye shield and completed the half-hour surgery. After he finished the last stitches, Sonia sat up and smiled. Through an interpreter, Anna explained the postoperative instructions. She handed her the package of dressings, antibiotics, and pain medications and gave her a hug. Then she felt sad that she might never see her again.

Several years later, while Anna was leading another medical missions team to MTM, they toured the village and noticed the church choir practicing. They took a few minutes to savor a native Creole song. Drawn to a lovely voice, Anna observed a young lady in the front row with a horizontal scar on her neck. There right in front of her stood Sonia!

As soon as the song was over, Anna rushed up to talk to her. She smiled proudly, displayed her scar, and told us about the past year. Physically, socially, and emotionally she responded well after surgery, and the cyst did not return. She had married and become a mother. Sonia experienced spiritual healing as well when she placed her faith in Jesus Christ. Her eyes sparkled when she told us how she and her husband actively participated in church work. Anna smiled as a great peace and comfort accompanied her as she headed back to the clinic. She had truly witnessed a miracle in Sonia's life.

Prayer

The medical teams that have come to visit have taken a number of different forms, depending on the training and experience of the individuals on the team, not just the doctors, but the entire team makeup is important. On some teams, there are designated Prayer Teams that work in the clinic doing nothing other than praying. They pray for the patients, doctors, the clinic as a whole, and everything related. During one trip, the prayer leader was Brian Pendleton, from the International House of Prayer in Kansas City. On the third day of clinic, the stress was beginning to build. Willem had started the clinic in the normal manner by gathering the team together outside, in front of the clinic, and opening with prayer with the long line of patients listening in. The team was tired, and with several days of work ahead, there was no break in the near future.

In the midmorning, the clinic was crowded with patients and a number of babies were screaming. The noise level overall was rising quickly. Brian looked over at a surgical procedure and asked how things were going, the doctor mentioned that the bleeding was steady and difficult to control and that the local anesthesia wasn't working very well, even though he had given more than normal. Brian took a walk through the clinic and assessed the overall situation, he remembered the steady beating of drums that he had heard the previous night, and he knew that something in the spiritual realm was going on there. Then he looked up and made eye contact with the surgeon from across the room. The doctor said, "Spend some time praising God." Brian immediately broke into a gentle sweet song of refreshing and then took a walk around the clinic praising God and intervening for the clinic.

At that point, Brian did battle. Not with flesh and blood but against rulers and powers of this dark world and against the spiritual forces of evil in the heavenly realms. God inhabits the praises of his people, by praising God and then praying and taking control, Brian had changed the spiritual environment. He came back into the clinic a few minutes later. He noticed that the babies were no longer crying, and it was quieter overall. He checked in with the surgery and asked if anything was different. While he hadn't done anything clinically but the bleeding had instantly stopped and the anesthetic was working again. Brian continued to intercede and made a powerful impact through his prayers.

Salt Distribution

Lymphatic filariasis is a terrible disease that causes grotesque swelling of the body, typically of people's legs, of women's breasts, and of men's genitals. In impoverished countries like Haiti, mosquitoes breed rampantly in pooled water, and most people don't have screens in their houses or mosquito nets around their beds to protect them from being bitten. The filarial parasite manifests it's infection and causes swelling that is aggravated by disastrous skin infections. The infections also cause eruptions that become putrid. The term elephantiasis describes the disfiguring symptoms that the disease brings.

It has been estimated that about one-quarter of the Haitian population is infected with the tiny, parasitic worms that cause lymphatic filariasis. Most infected Haitians have not yet developed symptoms and are not sick. But those who are symptomatic are badly disfigured, shunned, and cut off from normal social contact and jobs. A common belief is that people with elephantiasis have been victims of a voodoo curse. While the disease isn't fatal, it certainly hinders people's ability to function. Affected men who have been branded "town monsters" because of their appearance with terribly swollen limbs and their foul odor.

Mass treatment with diethylcarbamazine (DEC)-medicated salt has been used in a number of places as a control measure for lymphatic filariasis. Scientists at Notre Dame University, backed by the World Health Organization and U.S. Centers for Disease Control and Prevention, received a boost in early 2000 when the Bill and Melinda Gates Foundation awarded a grant to lay the groundwork for a campaign to eliminate lymphatic filariasis in Haiti. Simply switching out their regular salt with the DEC fortified salt prevents filariasis without altering the food's taste at all.

MTM has been a part of the solution to this problem by becoming a distribution center for the fortified salt. The village of Gramothe, including MTM's schools, use the fortified salt on a regular basis. In addition, patients who come to the clinic from far away receive a supply of salt as well. By treating infections with anti-parasitic medication and prevention of further infection using the fortified salt, filarial infections are being fought in every way possible.

Get Me a Hospital!

Willem welcomed a visiting medical team to his home and gave them the normal speech about the rules of the ministry including how the team is not to give out their names or any gifts to the locals. He paused and said, "A little while ago, I was driving in Port-au-Prince, and I heard a man screaming 'There he is, that's him!' And he was pointing right at me! There were political problems going on, and I was afraid that they were accusing me of being involved in all that. Since there was a lot of traffic, I couldn't go anywhere, and he came running right up to me and quickly took off his shirt and showed me a scar on the side of his chest," Willem laughed at the absurdity of the situation. "Then he gathered several of his friends around the car and told the story of the tumor on his side that Dr. Joe Fuller removed for him last year. At that point, I was beginning to breathe easier since I knew that he wasn't mad at me but wanted to thank me."

Willem looked over and asked Dr. Fuller if he remembered the patient. He replied, "We saw a lot of people and did a lot of surgeries, and I really can't recall."

"Well, he definitely remembers you," Willem continued. "This man told me that he had been to lots of clinics all over and nobody would help him without payment up front. We were able to provide a surgery for him that changed his life!" Willem looked at Dr. Fuller and said, "Your work makes a huge difference for the patients you see here. We are very glad you are here and look forward to another successful clinic."

Dr. Fuller was eager to help but knew the limitations of doing surgery in a clinic on a remote mountain. While Willem continued his welcome, his thoughts drifted off to hospitals in Haiti. Businessmen run a typical hospital in Haiti as a fee for service operation. Doctors rarely actually see the patients in the facility, medications and supplies are scarce, nursing care is rudimentary, and inpatients are essentially fed and cared for only by their family. The resulting care is poor, and the some hospitals have even gained the reputation as a place where you take the infirmed to die.

The operating room facilities are scheduled for local doctors on a regular basis and are occasionally used by missionary organizations. It's not uncommon for a visiting American doctor to perform a surgery and watch over the patient until he is discharged. But then when the visiting doctor has gone home, the patients receive a bill from the hospital not only for the hospital stay but also for the surgical fee. It doesn't seem to matter that the service was provided at no charge by volunteer surgeons separate from the hospital to the billing department.

Many patients only require medications for their treatment, but some require surgical intervention or hospitalization. MTM's clinic has been a host for a variety of surgical treatments that can be done under local anesthesia, but if general anesthesia is required, a hospital setting is necessary. The patients who needed advanced surgical care continued to pour into the clinic and doctors have been limited by the facilities.

Therefore, understanding the need for a reliable hospital with a higher standard, Willem broke ground on the new MTM surgical center when a donation was made for that purpose. Still in process, the hospital should be completed soon and promises to be the most complex project yet for MTM. The hospital, which will be open seven days a week, will employ a full-time Haitian doctor and at least two full-time nurses to provide continual care. When complete, this mountain hospital will look much like a same-day surgery center with overnight bays. It will allow teams to do much more extensive surgeries and medical care for the patients who desperately need it.

Progress

A team of nurse practitioners has already made progress toward providing comprehensive care has volunteered numerous times. Each visit gets more and more involved. They instituted an immunization program that is coordinated through the school and this will have a huge affect on the health and wellness of thousands of children.

Over the course of the ten years that MTM has been in operation, the medical clinic has had visiting teams at work as often as possible. Each week that the clinic is open, anywhere between 300 and 700 patients are seen and treated. Overall, tens of thousands of patients have received care. A wide variety of medical specialists have volunteered their time and talents for patient care in the clinic. Nurse practitioners, physician assistants, a variety of doctors, including family practice, internal medicine, urology, general surgery, and ophthalmology have treated patients. In addition, dentists, physical therapists, occupational therapists, and pharmacists have also pitched in. On occasion, a team will also conduct a mobile clinic at an even more remote location for patients unable to make the trip to Gramothe. Every trip also requires the assistance of numerous auxiliary personnel. Checking patients in, taking vital signs, recording medical data, fitting glasses, giving out gifts to children, and ever present chore of clean up are done by wonderful volunteers (age four to eighty-four) who make up the heart and soul of every medical mission team.

CHAPTER 10
A PLACE CALLED HOME

*Build houses and settle down; plant gardens
and eat what they produce.*

Jeremiah 29:5

Worship Jesus and Voodoo?

Lima Tilus was a Gramothe church member who had previously been a life-long dedicated voodoo follower. His experience was a life-changing decision he made at the heart level very much like Willem's own conversion. One Sunday after the church service, Lima stayed late and asked Willem some deep questions about Jesus and how to sincerely follow God's path. While not a voodoo priest himself, he had a profound respect for his religious heritage and wanted to honor it even after he had come to a decision for Christ. Willem listened to his heart and walked with Lima to his home as they discussed who Jesus was and that Jesus is the way, the truth, and the life. As they approached his home, Lima asked Willem a challenging question, "What is the best way that I should worship Jesus along with the other voodoo spirits?"

This question, in one form or another, was a common one and had been a problem for Christian missionaries to Haiti for generations. The Haitians understood the gospel and then incorporated Jesus into their list of spirits to worship. If the missionaries didn't recognize what they were doing, the practice of voodoo would continue to flourish within the church. In fact, many churches had unknowingly allowed their entire congregation to continue practicing voodoo even while they proclaimed to be Christians. Willem was well aware of this issue having witnessed it firsthand in his previous missionary experiences.

Lima's House

Willem understood his friend's genuine curiosity. He looked directly at Lima and repeated, "How should I worship Jesus along with the other voodoo spirits? I'm glad you asked." Willem sighed and walked over to Lima's house. The home was just a stone's throw from the church. The ten-by-fourteen-foot hut had been built and rebuilt piecemeal over the years from stone, plywood, corrugated steel, and whatever Lima could acquire. Willem stepped inside and saw one dirty bed without sheets and various pieces of clothing strewn across the dirt floor. There were no windows and no door. Lima's children slept wherever they could because they could not all fit on the bed at the same time. Termites had eaten numerous holes in the plywood walls, which were literally crumbling around them. The air was thick with a musty odor. A pair of brown rats scurried back and forth in the one-room shack. Willem stepped back outside drew a fresh breath. He saw the nearby cooking hut with the fire pit inside, and a few well-worn rocks that had been used as chairs for generations. He sat down on one of the rocks and looked over at the home.

Lima's five-year-old son Benjamin walked over to Willem and crawled up in his lap. "Good morning, little man," Willem said, grinning widely at the boy. Benjamin smiled back and gave him a big hug. He was barefoot and wore dirty brown shorts and a blue shirt with a hole in the left shoulder. Willem saw bleeding, red sores on his toes. He returned the hug and asked Lima about his son's feet.

"It's from the rats. I've tried everything, but I can't get rid of them," Lima answered. "They chew on all the children's feet at night, and the kids don't even wake up," he wiped away a tear from his eye as he spoke.

Willem set the boy down and watched him walk away; he turned to Lima and said, "Let me see if I can answer your question about worshiping God and voodoo. But first," Willem turned toward Lima's house and continued, "do you want to get rid of the rats?"

"Of course I do" Lima replied.

"Then you need a new house." Willem said with a grin.

"But how can I do that? I've tried everything I can." Lima replied.

"Will you and your family help with the work if I find a way to build you a new house?" Willem asked.

"Absolutely!"

"Give me some time, and we'll get this done." Willem replied. Then he turned and began heading back down the mountain.

"What were you going to tell me about voodoo?" Lima asked.

"That will come when we get rid of the rats." Willem answered and began walking toward his home. He was already formulating plans to build Lima a new home. Willem knew he could build him a home that was considerably larger so all the kids could have a place to sleep. Before he reached his house, he had estimated the supplies it would take and how much the whole project would cost. Willem called his loyal supporter Barry Cowan in the States to tell him the story.

"You remember our friend Lima from the village? He lives just up the hill from the church," Willem asked.

"Yes, a skinny man with a big smile with a bunch of kids—nine or so," Barry replied. "He's even recently given his heart to Jesus if I remember right."

"That's him." Willem replied. "His house is tragic. The walls are rotting away, the children have no place to sleep, and it is infested with rats. You might not believe this, but the rats actually eat at the children's toes at night." Willem paused to let that sink in for a moment then he continued, "We need to build Lima and new house and get rid of the rats."

"Let's build him a new house. What do you need?" Barry responded.

"I think we can do it for $3,500," Willem responded.

"Are you kidding? You can't even tear down a garage for that in the States! What kind of house will you build?" Barry inquired.

Willem explained, "Lima has lived all his life there in that hut. It's all he knows. If we build him an American style five-bedroom house with a kitchen, it will be too much of a jump for his family to manage and completely unfair to the rest of the village. We can build him a small house that is better than what he has right now, but he and his family will have to help us build it. That way it will be their home, and not a home that was given to them by anyone. It will be simple so that they can manage, and it will be a great improvement over the old house. But most importantly, it will be theirs to care for and free of rats."

"We'll get you the funds as soon as we can," Barry replied.

A Village Effort

With the money in his pocket, Willem went to town accompanied by Lima and his older sons. They purchased the materials they would need and loaded the bags of cement, rebar, cinder blocks, and all the other supplies into the truck. It took several trips going from the various supply stores in the city all the way back to the village, but they did it joyfully and with lots of anticipation.

Willem hired his team of four construction workers whom he had used on many other building projects; they were the skilled and reliable team. Willem also required that Lima, his family, and the entire village help in every stage of the process. This way the construction team had many hands to do the work. Equipped with shovels, axes, pickaxes, spades, and a variety of other equipment stacked a few yards from the site they assembled at Lima's house. Willem began the groundbreaking with prayer in Creole. He said, "Dear Jesus, we are yours, and all we have is yours. Let your new house be built here with your blessing. Please help this construction project go quickly and smoothly without injury or delay. Let your glory be displayed at all times as we work. Amen."

Willem explained the building plans to the team and let them get to work. With the house empty of all the family's possessions, they tore down the old place in a matter of minutes. The demolition liberated a large nest of rats seven to ten inches long with tails of equal length. They were quick and ran between the piles of wooden boards and steel, which now lay on the ground and became a maze for the rats to hide in. The team used their shovels, spades, and anything else they could to put an end to the rats one at a time. It was a comical site as they attacked the rodents but were afraid of getting too close or being bitten by them. Over the next fifteen minutes or so, several rats met their demise, and the rest escaped into the surrounding brush. The team cleared the debris and work continued.

They leveled a foundation and poured a concrete slab. The technical work was done with accuracy from the experienced builders, and the family helped by providing muscle power wherever possible. While Lima's younger children hauled water and sand, he helped by mixing the concrete, and his older boys took the concrete to the house bucket by bucket. Just like the in construction of the church, the entire village showed up. More than sixty willing volunteers showed up to haul water, sand, and equipment. Lima was pleased to see Willem hauling sand right along everyone else. Within a few days, the house began taking shape. Over the next few weeks they worked continuously. They built cinder block walls, poured a concrete roof, and installed a door and several windows. At the end of each day, the construction guys took time to share a few laughs with Lima's kids.

Extreme Makeover

After a number of weeks of labor from the team and the whole family, the house was complete, and Lima's family moved in to their new home. They had just experienced an *Extreme Home Makeover,* Haitian style. Strong cinderblock walls supported the solid concrete roof to provide a safe protected home that will keep the weather and animals outside. For the first time in this simple two-bedroom house with glass windows, a porch, the whole family had a place to sleep. There was no wood used in the construction. This prevented problems with termites and wood rot in the warm tropical weather. The cooking would still be done in a small cooking hut outside and a latrine was outside. By American standards it was a very rudimentary home, but to

Lima and his family it was a wonderful answer to prayer. But most importantly, it was clean and free of rats.

They held a party to celebrate when it's done. Lima's wife made food for everybody to say thank you. Willem looked over at Lima's wife and saw that she was sweeping up some concrete dust. She had a huge smile and said to Willem, "I'll keep this beautiful place clean."

Willem smiled back, "This home is not just a place to sleep in, it is a treasured possession that God has provided for you. It is your place of refuge and your home, so treat it with care. Wash the dishes right after each meal and keep your cooking area clean. Don't let them sit out because that brings roaches, ants, and other pests. Keep the kids clothes clean and give each child a bath before bed every night. The rats aren't really eating the kid's feet, but they eat the garbage and food that sticks to their feet. When the children are clean, the rats will leave them alone. You need to do these things because the rats will want to move back in and you must not let them."

Lima's wife maintained firm eye contact with Willem as he spoke. Nobody had ever told her this before. She had always simply accepted their infestations as part of life and had never considered it to be a result of lack of cleanliness in the home. But now, with Jesus as the center of their life, all of this had new meaning for her. She looked over her many children and back at Willem. "I will," she vowed.

Voodoo Out With the Rats

Willem shook the hands of the men on the construction team then Lima's family one by one, congratulating them on their strong work. With everybody still gathered around, he looked at Lima and said, "Voodoo is like the old house. It's full a bunch of spirits that are just like rats. You've seen the damage the rats do to your children. Voodoo does the same thing to our spirit. But God is a jealous God. He won't allow any voodoo at all in your life." Willem looked at him carefully as Lima stood motionless, listening intently. Willem continued, "When you follow Jesus, your heart is now a completely new house, and all the voodoo needs to be wiped out just like you wiped out the rats. This new heart Jesus gave you is beautiful and a great place for Jesus to live. Lima, you have to keep it clean and prevent any of the old voodoo from coming back in."

Lima looked around at his new home, his family, the construction team, and back at Willem. Everyone was intently focused on this lesson. He nodded and said, "I understand." He reached out and embraced Willem as tears of joy came down his face.

Willem embraced his friend, smiled, and said, "Jesus teaches about this in the ninth chapter of Matthew. He talks about wineskins and basically says the same thing." He held him by the shoulders at arms length and continued with a chuckle, "But I think this version works pretty well too." Lima learned many more aspects about his new life with Jesus and became one of the teachers in the church and has since become a deacon.

Six years later, when mission teams took tours through the village and visit his home, Lima proudly displayed his solid home. His family carefully scrubs each step that leads up to the porch, where he loves to sit and socialize with his neighbors. A one-by-three-foot solar panel on the roof charges a battery stored inside, which is used to power their radio and illuminate the home at night.

Family Building Continued

Willem has helped build over a dozen homes in Gramothe in a similar fashion. Each family was required to be involved in the construction, and the entire village chips in like an old-fashioned barn raising to make it a reality. This is a striking contrast to back biting and getting ahead, which is so common among people who struggle with poverty. When one individual does well, the others in the community tend to find a way to drag him down. With MTM's involvement, brotherly love and mutual respect derived from the love of Jesus Christ has brought a sense of cooperation to the village. One family gets the home, but the whole village had a hand in the building process.

In 2007, one family had funding and was ready to begin the work on their home. However, the adult sons refused to assist in the project. Without hesitation, Willem shut the project down and allowed the home to remain in disrepair. He explained, "If the sons will not cooperate now, this speaks volumes about their lack of respect for their father. And, if no cooperation is shown now, then will they cooperate when it is time to divide up the inheritance?" For them it was better to stop the project in its infantile stage than to build a home that would cause disunity and dissention in the family.

But for most of the families, however, the new home is completed with hard work and true joy. The costs of materials have more than doubled in the past few years, but since the majority of the work is done by family members, labor costs are minimal it's still possible to build a new home for a Haitian family for about $10,000.

Recently, Gramothe farmers have been able to turn a profit on their fields and build up a modest savings account. A few families have managed to not only maintain their new concrete home, but they have been able to build additions to their homes. These ambitious families have built additional rooms, indoor kitchens, and even expanded their porches. Meanwhile, throughout the village many other families are just getting started in the process and still need replacement of the walls that are crumbling around them.

CHAPTER 11
HOOPS!

A man can do nothing better than to eat and drink and find satisfaction in his work. This too, I see, is from the hand of God, for without him, who can eat or find enjoyment?

Ecclesiastes 2:24-25

All work and no play will make Gramothe a dull village. The region had seen plenty of work during the continuous construction projects since the foundation for the school was laid and had no shortage of work ahead of them. Willem wanted to bring some fun to the region as well. While soccer is the most popular sport in Haiti, there simply wasn't room for a soccer field in the early stages of the school development. The hillside did have one area that had been graded and was used for just about every purpose imaginable: a concrete mixing area, a parking lot, a playground, a market for local vendors, et cetera. This plot of land would work just fine for a basketball court. Since basketball was also pretty popular and a great option for the school, Willem decided to build a basketball court right there, next to the church and school.

Roger Stroup was excited about this prospect and mentioned it to some of his friends back home in Danville, Indiana. One evening, he stayed after son's basketball practice and chatted with the coach, David Moore. During the course of the conversation, the subject of a basketball court in Haiti came up and

David was eager to help. A couple of days later, he announced to the basketball team that they would be putting on a fund-raiser to raise money to build the court. After a successful campaign, Willem used those funds and put his construction crew to work. They poured a concrete slab and made it level and smooth, and they added regulation size baskets with breakaway rims. When the concrete had cured, and kids took to the court, Willem was thrilled. This was the first real recreation facility the village had ever had.

Willem e-mailed pictures of the new basketball court to Roger and asked him about putting on a basketball clinic in Gramothe. Roger talked to David over coffee, "You'll never believe it. They built the basketball court with the money you raised!"

David said, "Terrific!" and he gave Roger a high five.

"The kids love the court, and they even have some basketballs, but nobody knows the fundamentals of the game. If we brought in a group of guys who could coach them, it would make a world of difference," Roger proposed.

Without hesitation David replied, "I'd love to help. When should we go?"

In September of 2004, Roger, David, and two other coaches and went to Haiti to teach basketball. They traveled down with their shorts, basketball shoes, and a bag full of balls, quite different from every other mission team that had come before them. With Willem as their interpreter and teammate they held a basketball clinic for the village.

David recalled, "When we got there, the court was in good shape but had some debris on it. They had been using it like a multipurpose area with tables and other things on it, which you'd expect with a nice slab of concrete in a place like that. As I looked around, I saw kids running all over the court pushing trashcan lids or other round metal discs with a stick. There were a few other kids kicking around a soup can as if it were a soccer ball. Our first order of business was to make it look like a regulation court. We cleaned it up and painted the arc, the half court line and all the boundaries."

David explained, "We brought a bunch of balls and started by inviting the kids in gym class and those in recess at the school. On Monday we had about twenty or thirty kids, and then more showed up the next day. When we started out, we had a little trouble getting organized, but they picked up the skills very quickly. By the end of the week, we had over forty kids and a handful of adults running drills. These guys had no previous experience with the sport, but their attitude was terrific." The coaches organized the kids into pairs and started passing drills. This gave way to dribbling drills and individualized instruction on shooting technique. The kids were natural athletes, and after some time, they moved on to basic offense and defense. For four days, David and his small crew repeated drills. They saw quick progress and enjoyed the game with their new friends. A few people even gathered on the hillside to watch.

Just a few feet past the out of bounds line there was a steep drop-off down the mountain. Every now and then when someone would miss a pass, the ball would go out of bounds and down, down, down it went. The Americans simply stopped playing and looked for a new ball. But not the Haitian kids, one of them would disappear down the precipice and with the catlike agility bound down to retrieve the ball.

As the week came to an end, David was pleased with the progress they had made. "We had scrimmaged and gotten the idea of real basketball across to a group of people who wanted to learn, listen, and understand." But the kids had never had a real game, and the village had yet seen a real basketball game.

Petionville had the bragging rights that their basketball team was the best in Haiti. The team had banded together for the last couple of years and took on all comers. After a significant winning streak, they proclaimed themselves the Haitian National Basketball Team. Willem figured that this team would be the perfect opponent for the visiting coaches and asked them if they were up for an international challenge.

"Of course, we are! We're undefeated, and welcome anyone who would like to be beaten by some real talent," they said.

Willem passed the word on to David, informed him that the gauntlet had been thrown down, and they had a game on their hands. David looked around at his coaching staff and said, "I guess this is our team—the four of us plus Willem." David recalled, "You could tell Willem had played organized ball before based on his fundamental skills."

On Friday afternoon after the final drills, they brought the kids together and gave them some final coaching tips. They congratulated the kids on their improvement over the week and encouraged them to keep working on their game. When the players were dismissed, the Indiana coaching staff was shooting around, and they noticed a small crowd beginning for form along the side of the school. Word spread quickly through the village and excitement grew about the game. The Haitian National Basketball Team arrived at about noon and greeted the Americans warmly. They were a rag-tag group of young men, and none could have been more than twenty-three years old. They all shook hands and Willem spent a little time with them welcoming them to the village and gave them a brief tour. They settled on some arrangements and agreed on a timekeeper, score keeper, and referee. They were to play several games, and the best two out of three would be the winner. The crowd grew to several hundred excited fans cheering on the home team. No longer would they be doing drills and a little scrimmaging, a real game was developing before their very eyes.

As the first game got under way, the Haitian National Team took the court with a cockiness of a team that was not used to having a real challenge. They had the advantage of youth and energy on their side but lacked the experience of the many years of organized basketball that their opponents had. The game was incredibly physical. The Haitian team pushed and tripped in a physical way that would have started fists flying on most American black tops. They thought nothing of a shove in the back or grabbing their opponent's arm as they set a pick. The style took the Americans by surprise, and the Haitian team jumped out to an early lead.

Coach David called a timeout and gathered the team together, "Looks like we're got our hands full out there," he said with a grin. "Let's maintain good fundamentals. When we get pushed, don't push back but play our game. In time, we can take these young guys." They looked at one another, shrugged their shoulders, and turned back to the court. At the end of the first game they came up short.

When the second game started, the crowd had become more educated in the sport of basketball and with each basket the

Americans made, the crowd grew in excitement, which energized the team and put wide smiles on their faces. Conversely, the Haitian team struggled to gain a rhythm and resorted to further physical play. The Americans took the second game, and it was tied one to one; the final game would determine the winner. For the third and final game the Americans maintained their composure and played a clean game and came out victorious. At the game-ending whistle, the hillside full of people became a mass of people that flooded the court. They celebrated late into the night and the whole village thoroughly enjoyed their victory.

A few of the players that were in the basketball clinic became coaches who continued to coach and play basketball in the school. David summarized the experience saying, "I'll never forget it. I went up there to help and teach but was taught so much by the kids who were there. I'd love to go back and do it again."

CHAPTER 12
GIFTS OF ALL SIZES

Therefore, I urge you, brothers, in view of God's mercy, to offer your bodies as living sacrifices, holy and pleasing to God—this is your spiritual act of worship.

Romans 12:1

What does $51.34 buy?

Abigail began coming to MTM with her family on annual visits at the age of six. On each trip she assumed more responsibility as she helped in the clinic. On her first trip, her main responsibility was to play with the other children and get things for the adults as they were needed. After a few years, she learned to take blood pressures, administer pregnancy tests, and provide scabies treatments; she was willing to do just about anything she was asked to do.

When she was eight-years-old, Abigail stood in her basement and looked over the boxes of drugs and medical supplies as her family prepared to go on one of their trips. She saw her parents looking over some paperwork and overheard them talking about the cost of the supplies. She looked up and quietly asked her parents how much money she had in her bank account. They took a few minutes, looked it up, and reported the grand total of $51.34.

Abigail said, "I want to use that money to buy gifts for the kids who go to the clinic."

"That's your money, and you can do what you want with it. How much of it do you want to give?" Her mother asked.

"All of it," she replied.

With a tear in her eye, her mother e-mailed the MTM office and asked for a wish list of items that would be good gifts for the kids. Abigail took her $51.34 and went shopping with her mom for high-quality toys without moving parts that would last. After a successful shopping trip, she packed all the toys in a suitcase, which weighed in at the airline limit of fifty pounds.

When they arrived in Haiti, Abigail took special care of her personal items and proudly held her suitcase of gifts. Each morning the team had a Bible study before they left for the clinic. On the first morning the team leader read the words Jesus spoke in Matthew 6:1-4:

"Be careful not to do your acts of righteousness before men, to be seen by them. If you do, you will have no reward from your father in heaven. So when you give to the needy, do not announce it with trumpets, as the hypocrites do in the synagogues and on the streets, to be honored by men. I tell you the truth, they have received their reward in full. But when you give to the needy, do not let your left hand know what your right hand is doing, so that you're giving may be in secret. Then your father, who sees what is done in secret, will reward you."

The team had a meaningful discussion about what it meant to give so that you can be seen, as opposed to giving in private so that only the Father above will know. Abigail pondered this for a while and came away with a new outlook for how she would give that day. As they departed for the clinic, she didn't let anyone else on the team know about her bag of gifts, but went to work as a humble servant. She received specific instructions from Willem and got right to work giving lovingly and discretely within the walls of the clinic (while also performing her other clinic duties). Whenever she saw a child, she kept track of them, noting how they acted and tried to guess what kind of toy would be best, for them. When they were ready to leave, she offered the toy with a smile. Hour after hour, day after day, she repeated this process until her suitcase was almost empty. A few containers of bubbles were all that remained on the last afternoon, and she found that she needed to demonstrate how to blow bubbles with the little stick in the bottle, since the Haitian kids had never seen this before.

When she returned home, her suitcase might have been empty, but her heart was full from serving in love. She had acted in the most generous way possible. Abigail gave every penny she had and gave personally and specifically to the children she cared for.

The Rodeo

Willem played soccer with a missionary friend named Danny Day, who with his wife, Suzie, had a ministry to the elite of Haiti, but they struggled with car trouble because of the toll taken by the treacherous Haitian roads. Even though the total number of miles driven may not be high, the wear and tear is much worse per month than on most vehicles under normal use in the States. Not only that, it can be very difficult to get a car fixed in Haiti. A reputable mechanic will probably not stock the parts needed, and he will ask you to get them on your own. It's not uncommon for vehicles to sit idle for months while repairs are under way. Danny and Suzie were having their share of trouble with their older vehicles that they relied on.

In 2003, Willem mentioned to some team members that he wanted a better vehicle to use for transporting teams to and from the airport and getting them up the mountain. "The young and adventurous kids don't mind bouncing around in the back of a pickup, but a lot of people really need something more secure. Our little Black Isuzu Rodeo is a fine vehicle and is working very well for us as our personal car, but it's not big enough for teams." When Willem visited the States a few months later he stayed at a number of peoples homes during the trip. One of his hosts, a former team member took Willem into his garage and showed him his late model Toyota Land Cruiser.

He said, "This vehicle was built for the mountains of Haiti not for the paved roads of the Midwest. I want you to have it." Willem was overwhelmed with gratitude and within a couple of months, they shipped the Land Cruiser down, and Willem began using it for all kinds of purposes up and down the mountain.

Willem visited his friends Danny and Suzie for lunch one Sunday afternoon, and they drove both the Rodeo and Land Cruiser over to their home. Willem remembered, "I showed Danny the new Land Cruiser and shared with him how much God has blessed our ministry with this car. He asked me if he could buy the Rodeo, which was still in good shape. I got into a little bargaining with him and we settled on $7,000. He said he had $5,000 now and would get the rest later. I said okay, but you make sure you give me all the money. You know, I was just messing with him. Then I gave him the key and said, 'It's yours—no cost.' God has blessed us with this car, and we want to turn around and be a blessing to someone in return."

It's certainly not a common occurrence for a Haitian native to give an American missionary a car, but Willem was pleased to do so. He explained, "God says in Romans chapter 12 to give the best of yourself. We are to offer ourselves as living sacrifices holy and pleasing to God. We are to give our best to him and that means in everything we do."

As the keys passed from Willem to Danny in a loving exchange, Willem's wife, Beth, looked on, her personal vehicle had just been given away. Willem laughed, "It's always easier to give away your wife's car than your own!"

Beth shook her head and agreed, "Willem and I may argue about a lot of things, but we never disagree when it comes to helping people, we just do it. We never shut our doors to anyone who is in need."

Both the Rodeo and the Land Cruiser have served their respective missionary organizations faithfully over the years and both still have life in them. It really didn't matter to him if he was an American or Haitian, white or black, rich or poor. This exchange of blessings offered an opportunity for Willem to be a blessing to someone in need and to give his best.

The Gift Trailer

As MTM gained a foothold in the village, one of the major strengths of the ministry was the mission teams that visited on a regular basis. Each team came with a vision and a purpose: paint the preschool, install the steeple, preach at the pastor's conference, et cetera. But while they were there, each team member saw a village with tremendous need using their own eyes. Many times this had led to creative ways to help.

David Jones was a supporter who sponsored children in the school and regularly traveled to help MTM with various projects. He was absolutely captivated by Willem's vision and when he saw the children running around barefoot wearing nothing more than rags his heart went out to them. When he returned from one of his trips, he gathered donations for Haiti through his church, and worked with a friend who had an idea to use semitrailers to ship large amounts of goods to MTM. They made announcements from the pulpit and encouraged all donations for Haiti to be brought in. They arranged to have everything transported down to Gramothe in one huge load. Since their physical needs were endless, no specific directions were given for the donations because all giving would be appreciated. As the donations arrived, David took them from the church and began loading the trailer. They came in large black trash bags, brown cardboard boxes, or simply stacked items that he placed in growing piles within the trailer. People gave old clothes, toys, lumber, used tires, an old manual sewing machine, and countless other items. A local tee shirt silkscreen company donated over a thousand misprinted shirts of all sizes. The initial interest was fantastic and other local pastors even offered to help.

David e-mailed Willem to tell him the good news. The benevolence of the churches in Indiana had already been well established, and Willem welcomed a trailer full of donations. Willem gave him an enthusiastic response, "We'd be blessed by your giving."

Willem announced to the village that he was bringing a large trailer full of donations from the United States. When people asked what was in the trailer, he just said, "Come and we'll all find out together." While he did not know the details of what was inside, he knew it was from the same Americans who had been so helpful thus far and was confident that it would be a blessing.

The Unveiling

When the trailer arrived, Willem rented a truck and along with two men from Gramothe went to the dock to pick it up. He spoke with the customs agents who managed the transactions and together they identified the trailer. The agents asked for a list of the contents of the trailer but Willem had none. He explained that these were simply donations for his church and that he needed to transport it to the village. They insisted on having a detailed list of everything that was inside and proceeded to climb up the back bumper and roll up the door to see what was inside. They took several boxes out and set them down in the parking lot and with clipboard in hand, began to make their way through the trailer.

The customs process in Haiti is nothing like what you find in a port in the United States. There were no fences or security. Dozens of people hung out nearby with constant hopes of being able to scavenge at any opportunity. When the trailer door opened, the area was swarmed with men who looked like they were there to help. As the contents of the truck piled up on the ground around the back of the trailer, one man helped by carrying a box handed off the trailer by the customs agent and instead of placing the box on the ground behind the pile, he ran off and disappeared down the road. Other men followed suit and boxes and bags were quickly scattering in all directions.

Willem approached aggressively and raised a commotion as he scared off a few would-be looters, but the customs agents who were in the trailer shouted him down. They maintained their dominance in the situation by opposing Willem, thus allowing some of the theft to continue. For about a half an hour the agents went through the contents of the trailer and scribed the majority of the items on their pages. Willem and his two men did their best to monitor the donations in silence until the inspection was completed. When they hopped down from their position of control, the customs agents handed the clipboard to Willem for him to sign; it included a "customs fee" for the trailer.

"No, no, no! There should be no fee for these items," Willem said, appalled. He opposed this strongly and appealed to their limited sense of altruism. He explained that everything in the trailer was going to the needy people in his village. Eventually, he managed to get the fee reduced but was still required to pay. Reluctantly, he signed the paper, paid the fee, and watched the agents walk off, leaving a mess in their wake. They repacked as quickly as possible to minimize further loss. Finally, with the door closed, they hooked up their truck and headed back up to Gramothe.

When the trailer was brought to a parking place just a short distance from the village, word traveled quickly. Men, women, and children came together in great anticipation for what would be in the massive gift box and smiling faces surrounded the trailer door. David Jones was also there for the delivery of the trailer. He and Willem pushed his way through the crowd and unlocked the latch; Willem gave it a pull but couldn't open the door. The warning so often heard and ignored "Contents may have shifted in transit" now had new meaning. So much had shifted that the door simply wouldn't give. After about twenty minutes of pulling, shimmying, budging, and jostling the door finally creaked open. A few boxes fell out with the opening of the doors and Willem climbed up the bumper and stepped inside.

Boxes were scattered haphazardly in the cavernous metal beast. Willem picked up a box and opened it up so the crowd could see. He reached in and picked up two old T-shirts. He flipped through the box, only to find more and more shirts and other clothes. He set the box aside and moved to another one; this one was slightly bigger and taped shut. He it sliced open making quick work of the tape job and inside were blue jeans and slacks. Willem moved the box aside, and people from the crowd took it and held up the clothes for all the people to see and their smiling faces were as gracious as they were patient.

He continued with other boxes and black garbage bags and found old shoes, towels, and clothes with each new box. Much of the lumber made it just fine and so did the sewing machine, but many of the toys were broken. In a short period of time, the majority of the boxes had been emptied, and the contents spread on the trailer floor and hard-packed dirt. Willem set up a system for fair an equitable disbursement of the gifts to families throughout the village and set two faithful men in charge.

David walked with Willem back to the house in silence. After a while, Willem looked over to the back porch and saw David leaning over the railing, agonizing over the process that had just taken place. The customs officials, the plunder, and the damage were all too much. Not only was it a waste of resources, with thousands of dollars spent in transporting, but the theft was devastating. They had to do this better next time. Willem and David resolved that day to always give their best.

New Resolve

Willem brainstormed over the next few weeks. He dreamed up a wish list for items they would love to have. Rather than seeing only what Gramothe was and had been in the past, he was envisioning what he would love for it to be, a thriving prosperous town serving as a model for the surrounding villages with resources and support to help them as well.

Willem remembered what Barry Cowen had said when he was there at his last visit about needing better electricity at the village. Their generator was weak and power was intermittent at best. Barry had peppered Willem with a lot of ideas but each one was more expensive and complicated than the last. At the time it looked like these big ideas were for down the road so Willem had sidelined those thoughts. But now, he was dreaming big. He imagined having a high-quality generator at the church and another one at the school.

He also thought about what Barry had said about getting better transportation. The walk back and forth from the Willem's guesthouse to the village was arduous. Willem personally made the trip several times a day to deal with issues that continually came up. It seemed like he was needed everywhere. With projects being built, he was the supervisor, and his input was often required several times a day before further progress could be made. But, he was also needed back at the house, at the airport, or in town. Either walking or taking the truck, the trip was long and slow; he simply needed a better way to get around. How great would be to have a couple of all terrain vehicles (ATVs) to make this trip quick and easy? If he could simply hop on an ATV and be at the village in a couple of minutes, he would be more productive with his time. It would also incredibly beneficial the mission teams as well. Usually, a team would plan on working on a single project all day long, but it was common for a team to separate midday and have a couple of people switch projects or come back early for one reason or another. By making the trip on ATVs it would be much more efficient, and more work would get done more quickly.

The list of grand items that they would love to have in Gramothe went on and on. If they were to obtain quality new items that would last, all the people in the village would benefit. Willem pondered this for a few weeks bringing in numerous variations of his ideas. Finally, with his list complete, he was ready to contact David and Barry with his plan.

The New Plan

Willem picked up the phone and called David. "I can't express how much I appreciate your friendship and commitment. How would you like to make a tremendous difference in the coming years?"

"Sounds good," he replied. "What do you have in mind?" Willem proceeded to share his vision of how he saw the village. Electricity would open up many options for the people and really was becoming a huge need. They required a high-powered generator. With electric lights, they could hold meetings at the church and school at night. They could have an electrical amplified system for music at the church. There was literally no end to the amount of new and better things that would be possible once they had a constant source of electricity at the village. Their conversation continued and moved on to other subjects including the water project, ATVs, and plumbing.

David and Barry got right to work and contacted Dave Smittson who had helped with the water project. Dave worked for Cummins, a manufacturer of industrial generators. As they spoke about the need for MTM to have electricity Dave agreed to supply one generator at wholesale cost and amazingly gave another one absolutely free. They contacted John Corpening and discussed the prospect of enhancing the village water project. John was eager to upgrade the water project. He had proposed two-inch piping to replace the one-inch line, to increase the water flow. John generously provided the tubing plus a storehouse of other plumbing materials for various other projects. He gave hot water heaters, toilets, and a variety of tools and supplies for installation and maintenance.

They also contacted the local ATV dealer who had met Willem when he had been in town the previous summer. While walking through the showroom floor, Barry shared the need MTM had for smaller transportation. The ATVs were perfect for MTM. Barry went on and on about the incredible impact they would have for the day-to-day function of the ministry. That night Barry e-mailed Willem to tell him about the donation of two new ATVs.

The Second Unveiling

Over the next couple of months they gathered all kinds of supplies that were on Willem's wish list and acquired another trailer. When the trailer had been shipped to Haiti, the scene with the customs agent was set to be repeated. This time, however, the paperwork was clean, and the officials gave a cursory exam to the trailer's contents and ushered Willem and his men right on through without a fee.

Hoards of people gathered when the trailer was brought to the village to see what would be inside. Willem unlatched the doors and stood with his hand on the handle and turned to the crowd. "I'm here today to let you know that you are valuable in the eyes of God." He looked into the crowd of people and said, "You are loved because you are God's wonderful children." He let the words hang in the air for a moment then he turned to open the door, which easily swung open.

Inside, the people could clearly see newly packaged items stacked neatly from floor to ceiling, nothing had shifted in the long journey. After they removed the initial layer of boxes, they could see the black piping for the water project. Cheers went up throughout the crowd!

Elation continued as each item that was unpacked. Tucked into various areas of the trailer were new tools, doors, windows, plumbing supplies, and food. Toward the front, in the most protected region of the trailer, sat a shiny brand new red Honda TRX 450 R Four Wheeler. Next to it sat an identical blue one. Perfect in size and power level for the multiple trips up to the village and back. There were also two large crates containing new high-power diesel generators as well as electrical supplies and tools. Everything an electrician would need to install electricity in the village for the first time was right there in the trailer. Willem announced, "The school and church will have constant electricity. We will have the same technology that they have in the city." Once again, cheers went up from the crowd.

They unpacked the trailer, and the lighter equipment was carried on the heads of men and women up to the village, while the heavier equipment was set aside for pickup trucks to deliver. When the last box was unloaded, Willem let out a sigh of relief knowing that the trailer had provided everything he had hoped for.

Volunteers worldwide have long struggled with donations. Well-meaning donors have even saved used tea bags to give to the missionaries thinking that they were helping in a great way. Yet when a missionary opens a box and finds the pile of used tea bags, the message that they hear is, "This is what you are worth to me." Willem has continually told people new to Mountain Top Ministries, "Always give your best." If you are going to give tea, then send a box of new tea bags. Even better, send $5 and trust them to buy quality tea with it. During the following years more gifts, including many more trailers, would be delivered. Each one carried new and much needed equipment for the village and delivered the message of God's unmatched love.

EPICENTER EPILOGUE

But the one who hears my words and does not put them into practice is like a man who built a house on the ground without a foundation. The moment the torrent struck that house, it collapsed and its destruction was complete.

Luke 6:49

"That's our last patient. Let's head home," Sue Walsh said after a long Tuesday at the Gramothe medical clinic. Sue is a pediatric nurse practitioner who teaches nursing to graduate students at the University of Illinois at Chicago and has led numerous teams to work in the Gramothe clinic. Her team of twenty-three doctors, nurse practitioners, nurses, and other personnel had endured their last day in their weeklong trip. They had countless stories of patients that had walked to the clinic for days with terrible afflictions. Sue had been there a number of times, and their team helped over 600 patients during the course of the week and while the stories were always similar, this type of trip would never be routine.

They were pleased with their work in the clinic and were ready for rest. The final patients received their medications from the busy pharmacy as the team packed up their bags and did a little final organization work of the clinic to prepare it for the next team. The trip back to Willem's home was casual, some went by four-wheeler, some in the back of a truck but a number of the women decided to take the trip slowly and walk home to take in the scenery and fresh air one final time. Sue and a couple of friends donned their backpacks and began the hike down to the riverbed. Suddenly, at 4:53 P.M. on Tuesday, January 12, 2010, the ground started shaking. Sue said, "The tremor caused many to lose their balance or to fall. The rocks tumbled from the sides of the mountain like an avalanche into the river bed."

They looked around and saw that each her friends were safe, and they rushed up the opposite side of the mountain to Willem's house to catch up with the remainder of the team. On the way, Sue saw destruction everywhere as homes crumbled onto the shifting earth. When they arrived back at the house, everybody was visibly shaken up, but there were no major injuries to the team members. "Other members of our team were back at the house also felt the quake with very strong tremors, causing the trees and the house to violently shake but there was no collapse. Several brick walls and houses tumbled in Thomassin and Gramothe, and many were severely injured."

Willem was standing outside the clinic when the earthquake struck. He recalled the traumatic incident with a chuckle, "When the ground started moving, I looked up and saw my house was moving back and forth. I just thought to myself, 'Look at how well I built my house!' Then as it kept on going, I just said, 'Oh, Lord please let this stop.'"

He took a quick walk around the neighborhood and was absolutely amazed by the extent of the destruction outside of his four walls. Everywhere he looked, buildings had crumbled to the ground. People were crushed and trapped inside shops, stores, and homes everywhere. Willem helped people wherever he could, dragging people from rubble while his phone rang again and again. Friends from Petionville reported that the destruction in the city was terrible. Another friend who was a hospital administrator reported that the hospital was already overwhelmed with trauma victims. Willem offered to help and promised to bring his doctors and medical team over to the hospital that very night.

Beth got on the phone and called a handful of their friends in the States, "Willem and I are fine. The boys are okay, and the team is fine. Our home is not damaged, but the devastation here is beyond description. Please pray for Haiti, and pray for our team because they will need stamina, wisdom, and strength to endure what will be before them tonight."

Sue's medical team swung into action. They made a quick trip back up to the clinic and gathered as many medical supplies as they could carry. They packed bandages, irrigating fluid, anesthetic, sutures, crutches, and any other items they thought they could use. They loaded the team up into a truck and headed up to the hospital to help. Buildings lay in ruins all along the route to the hospital, the streets were chaotic, and people were dazed and traumatized.

Meanwhile the church building was still standing in Gramothe and many from the village congregated there after dark and shared stories. Many homes in the village were damaged or destroyed, but most of the people were free from major injuries. They were scheduled to carry on a worship service since it was Tuesday evening. The deacons looked around and could find no reason to not worship God, so they fired up the generator. The music team began playing, and the church held a time of worship. The music could be heard across the valley as they praised God even in the very worst of times.

When the medical team arrived at the hospital the scene was like a war zone. The narrow cinder-block halls were full of people with injuries of every kind. Sue said, "We were working with one Haitian physician, a few nurses, and a few other volunteers in conditions that were extremely poorly equipped to handle day-to-day care, let alone an emergency such as this."

Injured people were crowded in the parking lot, the hallways, and treatment rooms all over the hospital where people sat on the chairs, exam tables, and lay on the floor desperate for help. Willem had plenty of experience with crowds of people wanting medical attention and understood the triage process. He walked through the crowd trying to get the worst injuries cared for first. Many had injuries that were obviously fatal; they were given water and moved to a separate room in the hospital while attention was focused on those they could save.

They very quickly ran out of supplies, but patients continued to pour in. Sue said, "We cut up scrubs to use for bandages used broom handles for splints, and used anything else we could find to stop bleeding." Through the night they saw patients and delivered care the best they could.

That night Beth blogged on the MTM Web site and reported that the team was exhausted and overwhelmed and she ask for continued prayers not just for their team but for all the people of Haiti in the aftermath of such a major catastrophe and tragedy. The next day Willem said, "Praise God we have a team here. We saved hundreds of people the first night that it happened. And I finally went to bed about 5:00 in the morning."

The following day, Willem began assessing the extent of the damage. Knowing that gas, food, and water would soon be in short supply, he decided to begin rationing everything immediately. He said, "I just walked down to Port-au-Prince. As someone in the church, you always read or teach about the end of the world and you always wonder 'What's that gonna look like?' But to me, going to Port-au-Prince, that's what it was to me."

The catastrophic earthquake had a magnitude of 7.0 on the Richter scale. The epicenter was approximately sixteen miles southeast from Port-au-Prince and only ten miles from Gramothe. This was the largest earthquake in the region in over 200 years. The ground was felt shaking in several surrounding countries, including Cuba, Jamaica, Venezuela, Puerto Rico, and the bordering country of Dominican Republic. There was major damage throughout Port-au-Prince and the surrounding areas. Many major landmarks were destroyed, including the presidential palace, the police station, and the Hotel Montana. The main prison in Port-au-Prince collapsed during the earthquake. Many prisoners escaped into the streets. Damage to the Port-au-Prince seaport included the collapse of cranes into the water, structural damage to the pier, and an oil spill. Rendering the facility unusable for immediate rescue operations.

A number of public figures died in the earthquake, including government officials, clergy members, and foreign civilian and military personnel working with the United Nations. The wounded were taken to hospitals in pickup trucks, wheelbarrows, and improvised stretchers. The Port-au-Prince morgue became overwhelmed with thousands of dead bodies that were laid outside on the streets and sidewalks. Within the first week, they were dumped in mass graves without ceremony. An estimated 430,000 people died in the earthquake and in the days that followed.

In spite of the danger and utter chaos, Willem went to Port-au-Prince. "I was walking down from my house all the way to Port-au-Prince walking on dead bodies all over the street, and babies and pregnant women and all kind of classes. You know and people are crying and asking for help and looking people straight in the eye, and you do not have an answer, you know. And also, the people who were in the hospital, and they were asking them to leave because there's nothing they can do."

An estimated one third of Port-au-Prince's three million people were left homeless. Through the nights following the earthquake, many people in Haiti slept in the streets, on sidewalks, or in makeshift shantytowns either because their houses had been destroyed, or they feared structures still standing would not withstand aftershocks. Even President Préval was unsure of where he was going to sleep after his home was destroyed. He slept in the streets the first night and found shelter in the airport the following day.

A number of the major hospitals had collapsed, killing untold numbers of previously sick or injured people. Willem said, "People who were already sick were just laying in the street. The hospitals asked them to leave because there was nothing they could give them. People everywhere are begging, 'Help me, help me.' This is one of the toughest times in my life."

Like many developing countries, Haiti had no building codes. Nor did she have the means to enforce them. It was unlikely many buildings would have stood through any kind of disaster. In fact, about one year before the historic earthquake, a school collapsed on its own one a beautiful sunny day. Structures are often raised wherever they can fit; some buildings were built on slopes with insufficient foundations or steel reinforcement. Willem reported, "Most schools in Haiti are down, completely, down flat on the ground. And I'm not that great of an engineer, but when I was building the buildings for MTM I never cut corners and put a lot of steel in them, and they are still standing." The church, the schools, and the clinic all remained standing after the quake.

Willem continued, "But I also thank God for keeping me alive and to make a difference in these people's live. But now the question for Haiti, you have people who are out of food. People are out of water. And people did not know what was going on, at least they could have begun rationing, but now we have a crisis here. There are things I'd like to question God and ask God why, but I will not do it. He still sees what's going on, and he still loves his people. He's gonna take care of them."

Relief Efforts

The night the earthquake struck, government officials, including Haiti's ambassador to the United States issued appeals for international aid. The response to the disaster was one of the largest relief efforts in history. At least twenty countries mobilized within days to provide manpower, supplies, and financial aid to Haiti.

The neighboring Dominican Republic was the first country to step up to the plate, easing tensions that have existed between the two countries since the nineteenth century. The Dominican team sent food, bottled water, and heavy machinery to remove the rubble. The hospitals and airports in Dominican Republic were made available to receive aid that would then be transported to Haiti. Eight Dominican mobile medical units and numerous trucks with canned food, kitchens and cooks who could prepare 100,000 meals per day traveled over the border to help.

The other foreign aid was slower in coming. Even though aid was on the way, it took a couple of days to mobilize since streets were clogged with debris and rubble, making it nearly impossible to distribute food, water, temporary shelter, and medical supplies. Ships were also unable to render aid because the port facilities had been too damaged. Many of the injured in the initial days after the earthquake did not have access to health care and died. Slow distribution of resources in the days after the earthquake resulted in violence, as groups attempting to dispense food and other aid were attacked. Aid vehicles were also attacked. Some people who were frustrated with the lack of aid made roadblocks out of dead bodies.

The day after the earthquake, President Barack Obama pledged $100 million to the aid effort for the stricken Caribbean country and pledged that the people of Haiti would not be forgotten. Medical aid for the Haiti earthquake became a military-style operation. The United States Coast Guard deployed helicopters and several aircraft and cutters to the region to aid in relief work and perform reconnaissance flights over Haiti, assessing the worst damaged areas. The Coast Guard Cutter *Forward* arrived in the waters off Port-au-Prince at about 8:00 A.M. on Wednesday, and together with a Maritime Intelligence Support Team began to assess the damage caused to the port.

Elements of the U.S. Army's 82nd Airborne Division were immediately deployed along with the aircraft carrier USS *Carl Vinson* and the hospital ship *Comfort* to assist in the humanitarian relief efforts. The Red Cross erected a temporary field hospital, mobile health units, and water and sanitation units.

At dawn on January 15th, just three days after the earthquake, the USS *Carl Vinson* pulled near to the Haitian coast and began deploying their helicopters. They had offloaded combat aircraft in order to provide increased space for relief supplies and an unusually large complement of nineteen helicopters The nuclear-powered aircraft carrier has the capacity to distill 400,000 gallons of potable water a day. During her first day, she transferred about 35,000 gallons to shore via Navy heavy-lift helicopters. The *Carl Vinson* also provided the medical, air transport, and food preparation facilities of a small city. They worked with hundreds of existing aid organizations to distribute 600,000 basic food packets and 100,000 ten-liter water containers.

With the death toll in the hundreds of thousands, and the majority of the buildings in complete disarray, Haiti was on its knees. Even with the massive effort to help, the situation continued to be desperate. A percentage of the three million people in Port-au-Prince did receive help, but there was simply no way to meet the food, water, and shelter needs of the millions who were desperate and dying. Unprecedented damage to the fragile country had been done.

Mme. Stephen

Mme. Stephen has been a part of the leadership of the church in Gramothe since the beginning. As the head cook at the Gramothe School, her strong faith and determination to help her own community has stood out. She has mentored and taught many in the village and has been like a mother to many people. Most of all, she has been Willem's right arm in the village. Always willing to help, she was faithful and able to accomplish a tremendous amount with the people in the village, yet she knew her limitations and never went beyond what she was asked to do.

Recently she fell extremely ill and was diagnosed with tuberculosis. American and Haitian doctors alike have treated her with all the appropriate medications for this terrible and devastating disease, but her condition continued to worsen. She stopped working, and Willem visited her in her home often, with encouraging words and sharing stories. When her condition had advanced to the point where she could barely stand, Willem took her to a hospital in Port-au-Prince to receive treatment. When they arrived at the hospital, Willem looked at the horrific conditions and knew he would have to bring her more supplies from her home. Later that day he made another trip, along with Mme. Stephen's brother and brought along some food, water, and a mattress for her to sleep on. Willem shared his grief with several friends in the states who had also grown to love Mme. Stephen over the years. And they made plans to come and visit as soon as her funeral time was announced.

The family continued to visit bringing food and caring for her in the hospital and surprisingly, after three weeks, Mme. Stephen was still alive but was too weak to walk from her bed to the nearby chair. On Tuesday, January 12, the earthquake shook the hospital and large portions of the building collapsed around her. Her sister was attending her at the time, and she tried to carry Mme. Stephen. Knowing that her sister would not be able to carry her body, this amazing woman rose up and somehow walked out of the hospital on her own as it tumbled down around her!

The family desperately searched for two days through the death and rubble that filled the streets of Port-au-Prince but were unable to locate her. Each time when they returned home without finding her, they reported to Willem not only about their search but everything else that they had seen and endured. Willem encouraged them to continue the search until all hope was gone.

Somehow Mme. Stephen and her sister had walked four miles to an area near the airport where they slept in the street. They had with them only a small amount of water and no food. On Thursday midday, they were finally able to phone Willem as the phone service returned to local cell phones.

Her brother went right away to find her. He searched late into the night through the mass of humanity. The following day he continued his quest and finally found his two beloved sisters on the side of a busy street where they had found shade as they huddled under a tarp. On Saturday, four days after the hospital crumbled, Mme. Stephen came home. Though she was very skinny and still very ill, Willem and Beth received her back with joy. Beth said, "As I cupped her face in my hands, she shone like the noonday sun, full of praise and wonder to the awesomeness of our God."

At the break of the following morning, Willem once again visited her in Gramothe. Mme. Stephen shared with him that she was so happy because she never thought she would ever get to see her home again; she loves her home! She was also overjoyed to see her beautiful children that she thought she would never again be with. She reflected on how blessed she was to have life and to once again be with her children in her home.

MTM's Response

Up in the mountains, in a small village not far from the Port-au-Prince, MTM was still standing. For ten years, Gramothe has been the recipient of blessing from this hard-working organization, which has provided education, clean water, jobs, and medical care. Not only did they receive the physical blessings, but the people of Gramothe were delivered from bondage in voodoo and gladly received the life changing gospel of Jesus Christ. This thriving village, with no voodoo temples, has been transformed into a place that proclaimed the gospel every day. Its buildings did not receive major damage, and the people were bruised but not beaten by the earthquake.

MTM was uniquely positioned to be a provider for the surrounding region of Thomassin. The women mobilized their school cafeteria to provide food for the needs of the surrounding villages and with an almost unlimited supply of clean drinking water, Gramothe could feed and provide water for thousands. Village leaders from numerous nearby villages petitioned Willem for food distribution, so he worked with a variety of relief organizations to deliver fifty-pound bags of rice all over the region. This was done with as much fairness and equality as possible as Willem and the village leaders made sure that they delivered one for each family in the village.

Rebuilding will be a long and slow process in Haiti. With the efforts of building the church, schools, and hospital, MTM stood equipped with heavy-duty construction trucks, plenty of equipment, and capable crews with extensive experience in construction. However, when the earthquake hit, not only were the normal buildings destroyed, there were problems with the cement factory and the sand quarry, the two most crucial building supplies were cut off. The cement factory was also damaged during the violent shaking, and the sand quarry had a collapse that buried trucks and workmen under the sand. The quarry was shut down, and the long involved process of sorting out that quarry began. Willem found a way to obtain sand from another quarry, much further away and more costly. Eventually, cement became available on a limited basis and several months after the disaster, re-building began.

MTM has always centered on the gospel of Jesus Christ. Not only will they meet the physical needs of the surrounding area but the spiritual needs as well. Discipleship training classes and pastoral experience have equipped about a dozen men in the church to step up and assume pastoral responsibilities as they bring the gospel of Jesus Christ to every household they touch.

Right after the earthquake Willem said, "Well right now we've been blessed with what happened, and the church is still standing. Our house, our homes, and our families are all okay, and we thank God for that."

Mountain Top Ministries continues to work as a resource that ignites a vision in the Haitian people for their country to recognize their true potential, so that they may take spiritual ownership of their nation to defeat generational poverty village by village.

MOUNTAIN TOP MINISTRIES

Vision statement:

Mountain Top Ministries exists as a resource that ignites a vision in the Haitian people for their country to recognize their true potential, so that they may take spiritual ownership of their nation to defeat generational poverty village by village.

Mission Statement:

Share the good news of Jesus Christ with the families in the village of Gramothe and the people of Haiti by providing for their spiritual, physical and academic needs.

MTMHaiti.com

Made in the USA
Charleston, SC
21 November 2010